C000121629

Start Your
Video Game Career

Jason W. Bay

Copyright © 2017 Jason W. Bay

All rights reserved.

ISBN: 0692920927
ISBN-13: 978-0-692-92092-3 (Game Industry Career Guide)

CONTENTS

Start Your Video Game Career

CHAPTER ONE
Introduction

I'll never forget the day I got my first video game console. It was a chilly Montana morning. I climbed out of bed and stumbled bleary-eyed to the living room, with plans to watch Saturday morning cartoons in my full-body Spider-Man pajamas. (Did I mention I was six years old?) As I turned toward the television, there it was: a brand-new Atari 2600 home video game system, in all of its beautiful faux-wood and black-plastic glory.

I immediately fell in love.

On that day, way back in 1980, I began my lifelong obsession with video games. In grade school, it was staying up past my bedtime for "just five more minutes" to finish a level (or two, or three). In college, it was skipping out on social events to binge on whichever new game had just been released. As an adult, it's shirking housework to burn entire weekends gunning through bandit camps with my wife Shawna. Gaming has given me so many memories, I wouldn't trade it for the world.

But even as I poured all that time, energy, and passion into playing games as a kid, it never occurred to me — not even once! — that it was possible to make games as a full-time job. Even as I sketched detailed schematics for science-fiction weapons during class, or spent my summers filling graph paper with complex maps for detailed Dungeons and Dragons campaigns, I never realized that I was accidentally preparing myself for a career in game development.

Fast-forward a decade or two. I landed my first video game job in 2001, and I've had many different job titles since then: QA Tester, Game Designer, Lead Programmer, Studio Technical Director, Product Manager, and Studio Head. I've spent years hiring, managing, and supporting game makers from varied backgrounds, and I've written for game industry magazines, spoken at international game industry events, and worked with top game development colleges and universities.

But I'm not telling you that to brag.

(Maybe just a little.)

I'm telling you because my mountain of experience has helped me understand exactly what it takes to get into the game industry, and exactly what it takes to succeed once you're there. I know what questions you want to ask, and I know how to answer them — or, in some cases, how to help you find your own answers, because each of us has unique talent and is following our own unique path.

My hope is that after you read this book, you'll have the knowledge and tools you need to succeed every step of the way — from choosing a career, to getting an education (either formally or informally), writing your résumé and portfolio, finding and applying for jobs, interviewing, and succeeding in a lifelong game development career. And I sincerely hope that you'll be more inspired than ever to pursue your dream job making video games.

There's no need to read the book cover to cover, if that's not your style. Feel free to skip around between chapters, or read just the sections that cover whichever stage of the journey you happen to be in right now. If you do skip around, I hope you'll come back whenever you need more guidance or advice. I'll be right here waiting for you.

Let's get started!

Could I really get a job making games?

Game development is the art and science of creating a video game — all the way from coming up with a game idea, to building the art and writing the code, to finding and fixing bugs, to launching the game so people can play it. You can use the term "game developer" to describe anybody who makes games, no matter what their specific job is on the game team.

If you're a student thinking about your future career, a job making video games might seem too good to be true. Also, your parents might be skeptical about whether game development is a "real job" with a salary that could support you and your future family.

The answer is easy: Yes, it's a real job. And yes, you can make a great living doing it.

To be fair, this wasn't the case twenty years ago — the game industry used to be tiny, and it was rare to get a job making games. But today, the video game industry is huge and it employs thousands of game developers around the world. Here are some important statistics to help you (and your parents) understand the massive scope of the game industry today:

- Total consumer spending on video games is over USD $70 billion annually. That's more than the movie and music industries combined, and it's growing each year.
- Over 60% of Americans play video games. That's more than the number of Americans who watch sports.
- The average gamer is thirty-one years old.

Games aren't just for kids. They're a daily part of mainstream life for millions of fans of all ages, and have created an enormous market for new games to be created and sold each year.

The industry is growing, with no signs of slowing, so it's likely to continue providing job opportunities for decades to come.

Someone needs to build all those new games. Why shouldn't it be you?

CHAPTER TWO
Choosing a career

When I was a kid, adults were always asking me, "What do you want to be when you grow up?" Adults love that question. I used to think they asked because they were legitimately interested in my choice of future career. But now that I'm an adult myself, I've come to realize they ask it for a different reason — they ask because most adults still don't know what *they* want to be when they grow up, either. They're locked into a job they don't like, in a career they don't love, so it's fun to live vicariously through young people who seem to have every fantastic option still open to them. It's charming, but also kind of sad.

What did I want to be when I grew up? Like you, I've had different answers over the years. Early on, I wanted to be a ventriloquist, because I got a ventriloquist dummy for my birthday one year and it was a fun toy. But then one day, a grown-up told me you can't make a living as a ventriloquist. That turns out not to be true, but I believed it at the time, so I came up with other answers: paleontologist, because I loved dinosaurs; cartographer, because I loved maps (and I loved how impressed grown-ups were when I used the word "cartographer"); magician, because I could do card tricks and I was pretty good at it. By the time I started college, I had my sights set on marine biology, because I loved the ocean and the mysterious creatures of the deep.

But the fact is, whether you're in grade school, high school, or even college, it may still be too early to know what you want to do when you grow up. Partly because you're still learning what you like and dislike, and what you're good at and not so good at. And partly because there are thousands of different jobs you haven't even heard of yet, so it's impossible to know which one might be right for your unique mix of talent and personality.

The video game industry is full of people who didn't know what they wanted to be when they grew up. Most of them are like me: they've been avid gamers their whole lives, but didn't know it could be a full-time career. I've worked with game developers who started out as accountants, restaurant waiters, movie theater managers, soldiers, auto mechanics, and teachers. But the game industry is also full of people who knew exactly what they wanted to do with their lives — they researched the various career options, chose one they thought would fit them best, then went to school to learn the right skills and graduated to get a job making games. My own career path was meandering, but many of the game artists, designers, programmers, audio engineers, producers, QA testers, and others in the game industry took a more direct route.

Whether your path into the game industry is like a high-speed raceway or, like mine, more of a dusty, meandering back road, it's best to start out by researching and understanding your options. The following section takes a look at some of the different career paths available to you, and offers advice to steer you in the right direction.

What are the main jobs in the game industry?

There are dozens of different job types in the game industry, with new ones cropping up every year as gaming and technology advance. But you can think about most of them as falling into a few discrete job "families," and learning a bit about each family is a good place to start.

Programmers. Also called coders, engineers, or developers. Programmers use a programming language like C++, C#, or Java, to instruct the computer on how to take all of the art and other content and turn it into a working game. Programming is by far the most technical job in the industry. Most programmers start by getting a degree in computer science, but if you're a good self-starter then you may be able to learn on your own and get an entry-level programming job at a game company. (I know many successful programmers who don't have a computer science degree, but it's a difficult way to start out.)

Artists. This job family includes job specialties such as animators, 3D modelers, concept artists, UI artists, and technical artists. Art is one of the hardest game jobs to get into, because you need strong artistic talent, plus you have to be skilled with complex art tools used to create digital content, such as Autodesk Maya and Adobe Photoshop. And you'll need to have assembled a great portfolio to showcase your skills. The good news is that there are many different kinds of art jobs in the video game industry, so if you're not good at one then you can try another. If you're just starting out, you might know that you love doing art but aren't sure which job is right for you. Going to an art school is a good way to try out different areas (and earn a degree while you're at it), but I also know many successful artists who are self-taught. If you're more interested in the visuals of games than the technical aspects, then a career as an artist might be a good fit.

Game Designers. This family includes game designers, level designers, and content designers. More than any other job in the game industry, a designer needs to have an incredibly broad and deep understanding of video games. You can only get that kind of insight from playing a ton of games, analyzing them, discussing them with other design-minded people and, eventually, by making your own games so you can learn through trial and error. If you're the kind of person who loves to analyze games and truly understand what makes them a big hit or a big flop, then this could be the job for you.

Audio Engineers. This family is made up of sound designers, sound engineers, audio implementers, and music composers. There are precious few audio jobs in the game industry, because just one audio engineer can often serve multiple game teams. In fact, it's common to have a single audio engineer covering an entire game studio. Many studios don't have any full-time audio staff at all, instead choosing to hire them on a temporary contractual basis as needed. You can contract through a staffing agency, or as an employee of a freelance audio firm. Most of the composers and audio engineers I've met are self-taught, although many attended audio engineering schools or have music-related university degrees.

Producers. Every team needs people whose job it is to guide and focus the developers, so they can concentrate on doing great work without worrying about other aspects of running a business. For a game team, that person is the producer. They're responsible for the daily planning and management of the team. At some studios, they're also responsible for shepherding the "vision" of the game. To be a successful producer, you need to have great planning skills and be a good communicator. It helps if you're good with numbers, since you may be managing budgets and other business metrics. There are many ways to start your career as a producer. Producers often start as game testers, where they learn the quality-control and iteration processes of game development before moving onto a team as an associate producer. It's common for game studios to have openings for production assistants, which is another good way to get started in a production job.

Game Testers. Let's start by busting a common myth: testers do not just "sit around and play games all day." It's real work. You'll be playing games that are under construction, well before they're finished. They'll be buggy and missing content and, at the early stages, they won't even be "playable" in any real sense. Testers play the latest under-construction version of the game, and report anything that looks bad or doesn't work right. It's an important role because if they don't do their jobs well, it leads to millions of disappointed fans as they realize the game has bugs, crashes, or (even worse) loses their progress. Testing jobs usually don't pay well, but starting your career as a tester is one of the easiest ways to break into the video game industry. I know many people who started as testers and then went on to become producers, artists, designers, or programmers. In fact, I started my career as a tester and later went on to run a large game studio. If you're interested, I also wrote a book about it, called Land a Job as a Video Game Tester.

Is it difficult to get a job at a video game company?

I'd love to be able to tell you, "Nope, it's not difficult at all. Anybody can get a job making games." Unfortunately, the real answer is that some game jobs are easy to get, but others are difficult. In fact, for some game jobs, it's nearly impossible to get hired as a full-time employee. Why are some so easy to get, while others are challenging?

First of all, some jobs are in higher demand by game teams. For example, most game teams need several artists, programmers, and testers, but only one or two writers, producers, marketers, and technical artists. Jobs that are rarer on game teams are harder to get because there are fewer positions available in the industry as a whole.

Another factor is that some jobs aren't needed by game teams all the way from start to finish. For example, concept artists are mostly needed at the beginning of the project, when the look and feel of the game's characters and levels are being fleshed out. But once those are established, the concept artist may no longer be needed by the game team. Similarly, audio engineers are often needed later in the game's production because their work depends on the game's animations and environments to be largely complete before they can create the audio and sound effects. For some of those jobs, the team might even hire temporary contractors rather than keep permanent employees on their payroll, which makes it even harder to find full-time jobs. Compare that to the game's programmers, who are needed very early in the development cycle and remain on the team all the way through to the end.

If you've already chosen a career path that you think is one of the rarer jobs like audio engineer or writer, don't let this scare you away — just make sure you're comfortable working as a contractor or temporary employee in case you can't find a permanent job right away.

Do game designers need to know how to code?

The very best game designers have a holistic ability in several other game jobs, and knowing how to do some programming is by far the most beneficial. But if you're really only interested in designing games, not programming them, then why is it so important to know how to write code?

For starters, everything in a video game is enabled by its programming. Artists make the art, designers construct the experience, and audio people whip up the music and sound effects, but it doesn't come alive as a game until a programmer writes the code that powers it all. As a game designer, much of your job is dependent on your game team's programmers — and your job will be much easier if you can collaborate with the programmers and know enough about coding to understand what they're talking about.

Understanding programming will also help you work more effectively within the game's technical limitations, and to brainstorm with programmers to explore creative approaches to design challenges. And, to be frank, some programmers can be a bit snobby towards people who aren't technical and don't understand code, so having some coding ability of your own can help you earn and keep the respect of your team's programmers.

Another reason to learn programming is that most modern game engines require game designers to write code using a scripting language. Scripting isn't like full-blown game programming — it's less complex, and not as powerful. But as a game designer, you'll use it to do powerful things like customizing your games, designing the artificial intelligence, controlling how the player interacts with the game world, and more.

Still not convinced? How about this: if you have some basic programming skills, then you should be able to use any of the modern game-making tools to build a game prototype, or even a complete game of your own. It's unlikely to be a large, professional looking triple-A game, but you could certainly make something you can be proud of. It's a lot of fun to make your own games, and it looks great on your résumé and game design portfolio when you apply for jobs.

Could being a game designer make me hate games?

What's your favorite food? Think about eating that food twenty times each day, year after year. It wouldn't take long before you never wanted to taste, see, or even *smell* your "favorite" food again — your love for that food would be forever curtailed. Some people are afraid that might happen if they were to become a game developer. If you love playing games, then why would you want a career that forced you to work with games day after day, year after year?

I've worked with hundreds of game developers over the years, and I've met only one who claimed he could no longer stand a particular genre of game after having made too many of them at his job. But he was generally a cranky guy, so I wouldn't take him too seriously — I'll bet he still plays. And speaking from my own experience, I've worked in the game industry for over fifteen years and I still love playing games of every kind.

However, there have been certain times in my past when I wasn't as into gaming as usual, and it directly correlates with the times when I was working weeks of overtime to meet a deadline — otherwise known as "crunch." There was one particularly crunchy project where I was working eighty-hour weeks, which didn't leave me with much energy (or time) to play games until the project was finished and my schedule was back to normal.

There was one other time when I didn't play games for almost a year. It was just after I was laid off from my job in 2013, as part of a large corporate downsizing. Around fifty great developers lost their jobs. It happened after some difficult years for the company, and was an emotional time for everybody involved. After that, I didn't play games for several months. Why did I stop playing? I'm not exactly sure. I think it was partly because I was busy applying and interviewing for new jobs, and partly because I was starting a new business (which ended up becoming the GameIndustryCareerGuide.com website and podcast). I think I just needed a break to focus on other things in my life. Fortunately, the dry spell didn't last long — I got back to gaming and I still love it. I'm more fired up about making and playing games now than ever.

Like most things in life, your interest in gaming will ebb and flow. In fact, I think you'll find that learning how to make games will give you more appreciation for gaming. Once you begin to grasp the vast amount of hard work and creativity that are required, you can't help but look at even the smallest games with a new appreciation and a deeper connection with the amazing skill of the artists, designers, coders and others who brought it to life. Just as studying songwriting or filmmaking can inspire a deeper love of music and movies, game development can take your love of gaming to a whole new level.

Do video game programmers get to contribute to game design?

Game programming and game design are two separate jobs, and they're quite different from one another. A programmer's job is to write the code that drives the game, and a designer's job is to conceive the game world and plan the player's interactions with the game's world and characters. But since the programmers are usually the ones implementing the design, they often have a high degree of influence on the outcome.

This is especially true for smaller game teams, because there are fewer dedicated designers and ideas tend to come from any and all team members. For example, the game programmer might need to design some of the enemy behaviors, or the environment artist might also be called on to do level design. Compare that to a larger triple-A game project with hundreds of team members, where most people are specialists and there's not much overlap between jobs. I know of one really big team that had an entire art group dedicated solely to making rocks and shrubs. Those artists certainly didn't have time to contribute to the game design.

Another factor that influences whether a programmer gets to contribute to the game's design is the type of programmer that you are and the areas of specialty that you bring to the team. If you're the game's combat programmer or artificial intelligence (AI) programmer, it's likely that you'll work closely with the designers to plan, implement and refine the game's player controls and combat mechanics. In fact, the best combat designers I know are also game programmers.

If you're not a design-facing programmer, then your level of contribution to the game's design boils down to this: How good of a game designer are you? As you work with your game team, over time you'll naturally contribute ideas to the group during meetings, email and chat, or impromptu hallway discussions. Some of your ideas will be good, and some of them won't. But if you seem to have a knack for good design, people on the team will notice. If you really want to have a say in the game's design, put some extra effort into study of game design, and contribute constructive ideas to your team whenever the opportunity arises.

Do game testers work a lot of overtime?

If the game team you're working for is mismanaged, then yes, it can lead to excessive overtime for the testers on the quality assurance (QA) team. When I was a tester, I usually worked a normal eight-hour day. But there were many times when I worked late into the night to help the QA team finish our test pass before sending the build to the publisher for approval.

If you don't want to work a lot of overtime, try to avoid working for poorly managed companies. Do some research and investigate any company before you accept a job offer, to find out about their work-life balance. You can also ask people during the job interview — ask them how often they crunch, and how many hours of overtime are typically required each week.

You could also search for anonymous employee reviews about the company on Glassdoor.com, or any discussion forum where game developers candidly discuss life at their companies. It's good information to have, but be sure to take it with a grain of salt — many of those reviews are posted by disgruntled ex-employees, so they tend to give an overly negative view of the company.

But let's be realistic: this is the game industry, so you won't be able to avoid overtime entirely. The goal is to keep it under control, so that your work-life balance stays balanced.

What are the downsides of a job testing video games?

If you've gone online and researched a career as a game tester, you may have found articles saying that game testing is a difficult and thankless job, or that testers aren't shown as much respect as other roles on the game team. Unfortunately, I think that's true at many game companies. But why?

It's partly because game testers don't typically have as much experience and education as other game industry employees. But I suspect the main reason is because testers are often hired as temporary employees, so they're like the redshirts on Star Trek — everybody knows they won't be around for long, so the full-timers don't bother to form close friendships with them. So if you get a game testing job on a contract or temporary basis, you might need to work harder to make friends with people on the game team. Don't wait for them to reach out to you — try talking to them during breaks, at lunchtime, and at after-work events. But don't forget, your primary team is the other testers in your group. Enjoy their company and don't sweat it if the developers on the game team take a while to warm up to you.

I started my own game career as a tester. I worked on projects that were fun and made me proud, and I also worked on projects that were mismanaged and run by developers that were jerks. But overall, game testing is great because you get to participate in the collaborative effort of making a video game. You get to work with highly talented people to make the greatest game you can make, and you get to feel great knowing that you played a key role in the game's success.

I think you'll find that the pros outweigh the cons by a landslide. Even after a rough day, you'll always be able to remind yourself that you spent the day doing what you loved. The icing on the cake is, of course, that you got paid to do it.

Do I need to be a good writer to get a job testing games?

You'll need a variety of skills to become a good game tester, and one of them is the ability to be a decent writer. However, there are several different kinds of writing, and you don't need to be good at all of them to succeed as a tester.

For example, you don't need to be a good creative writer. The ability to write characters, plots, and compelling stories is a skill that game designers and game writers use every day, but it's not a skill that's required of game testers.

However, testers do need to be good at technical writing. Technical writing is when you share information about a technical topic, or give specific and detailed instructions that somebody else needs to follow in order to accomplish steps toward a particular goal. As a game tester, you'll be spending a lot of your time doing technical writing, because one of your primary tasks is to write bug reports — and that's technical writing.

What exactly is a bug report? It's a short document that describes a bug that you found while testing the game. It provides a clear and concise description of the bug, along with detailed steps that the game development team can take to make the bug happen on their own computers. As a game tester, you'll write one bug report for each bug that you find — so if you find twelve bugs in a day of work, then you'll also write twelve bug reports.

Fortunately, bug reports aren't as long or as in-depth as book reports. They're short — often just a single paragraph plus your list of reproduction steps (called "repro steps" in tester lingo). But that doesn't mean they're easy to write. It can take a lot of practice to learn how to write bug reports that are clear and effective. So start improving your writing skills now, simply by writing more often. Start a blog or a Tumblr or a personal journal, and write in it regularly. The more you write, the better you'll get at writing.

How can I learn how to be a game writer?

For starters, if you haven't done much creative writing yet, what are you waiting for? If you have a computer — or even just a pen and paper —

then you already have the tools you need to start writing stories.

If you aren't sure how to start writing stories, there's a ton of help online. Do a search for "learn creative writing" and you'll find dozens of articles and tutorials. They'll help you get your creative juices flowing and give you a framework to start thinking about how to construct a narrative. You don't need to write stories for games just yet — focus on learning the basics of crafting a compelling story with interesting characters and dialogue. After that? Practice, practice, practice. The more creative writing you do, the better you'll get.

You can post your writing exercises to a blog online, or you could even turn them into an e-book and self-publish them on Amazon.com. The key is to start writing, finish some stories, and them get them out into the world.

You can hone your craft by getting feedback from your friends and family. Every story you write will be better than the last. Writing for games isn't much different than any other creative writing project, so keep writing, keep getting feedback from others, and keep improving. After you've built a collection of short stories and other writing projects, you can put your best work into a portfolio to show prospective employers and start applying for jobs as a game writer.

I already have a career, would I be crazy to switch to game dev?

If you're unhappy with your current career, there's nothing crazy about switching to the game industry. I've worked with people from dozens of backgrounds — accounting, web development, teachers, military — who switched to the game industry later in life.

In most countries, including the USA, people don't retire until they're over sixty years old. But the "good old days," when people worked for the same company their entire career, are long gone — it's become commonplace for a person to change careers several times over the course of their working life. So if your current job makes you miserable, and you still have ten or more years to spend in the workforce, then now is a good time to explore something new.

But you probably won't be able to switch to a completely different career right away. Once you're ready for a change, it will take time, effort, and patience to shift away from the career you're in now and start moving toward a new one in game development.

The biggest risk when switching careers is the danger of losing your comfortable income while you transition. That's why a good strategy is to stay at your current job for now, and start learning how to make games in your free time. It's a "self study" approach: take online classes, follow tutorials for the popular game engines such as Unity 3D or Amazon Lumberyard, and "learn by doing" with the support of online game development communities and forums.

You'll begin to learn the basics of game development. You'll get experience using the tools of the trade: the art tools, design tools, programming tools, and game engines. And you'll begin to learn the techniques and vocabulary of game development.

You'll also start building a portfolio of game demos. And once you have a portfolio of game development work that you've done, you'll have examples of your work that you can show potential employers when you start applying for entry-level jobs at game development studios. All the while, you can sleep comfortably knowing that you'll continue to receive a paycheck from your current job while you prepare for your new one.

Should I take a job I don't want, just to get my foot in the door?

When you're first trying to break into the game industry, there's a curious bit of advice you're likely hear. It goes like this: "Breaking into the game industry is hard. Start by taking a job that's easier to get, such as a QA job, just to get your foot in the door." That's a reasonable strategy in some cases, but is it the right strategy for you?

Not if you already have the skills you need to get hired, and if you have a strong portfolio. Like any job hunt, it might take a few weeks or even a few months before you get hired, but if you've got what it takes then there's little reason to settle for less. On the other hand, if you don't have the skills you need to get hired in the job you want, or if you don't have a strong enough portfolio, then taking a different job has some advantages (besides the obvious paycheck).

First of all, working in a game studio will give you a crash course in the game development process. Even if you're already familiar with game development from school or personal projects, the process looks very different when scaled up to a team of dozens of developers on a multi-year triple-A game project. You'll begin to learn all about that process, no matter which job you take at the game studio.

The second reason is that you'll start meeting experienced game developers, and you'll have opportunities to learn from them because people in the game industry are often friendly and eager to mentor newbies. Not only is that a good way to build your network, it's also a great way to quickly grow your skills by learning from professionals.

A third reason is because once you're an insider, you'll hear about new job openings in the company — even before they get posted to the public. Most studios prefer to hire people they already know and trust from inside the company, rather than rolling the dice with an outsider. So if you've been building your skills and your portfolio while you're working there, and if you've been hanging out with the professionals and learning from them, then one day you might be the right person to fill a new job opening.

Those are some good reasons in favor of taking the job. But what are the reasons you might not want to take it?

The main reason is that working every day at a job you don't like is a painful way to spend a couple of years. If you take a job as a game tester, for example, and you end up hating it, then those eight-hour days are going to feel like soul-crushing eighty-hour days.

But my guess is that you'll be so busy learning about game development, building new skills, and meeting cool people who can help you, that the time will fly by. And before you know it, you might get an opportunity to move into the job that you really want, or maybe even a job you didn't know existed. If there's one thing I can tell you about a career in games, it's that you never know exactly where it could take you.

What if game development isn't for me?

There's only one way to find out whether you'd enjoy a career in game development: start doing game development. It doesn't take a huge time commitment, just start doing it as a hobby and see where it takes you.

Once you spend several hours learning about game development and building one or two small game demos, it's possible that you'll decide it's not really for you. Maybe you enjoy playing games, but making them doesn't turn out to be as appealing as you expected. Maybe game development just doesn't "click" with you.

Or, maybe game development does click with you, but as a hobby instead of a full-time job. Maybe you enjoy making indie games by yourself or with friends, because it de-stresses you and sends you back to your day job feeling refreshed each week.

Or, maybe your day job truly is miserable, and you do need to get out as soon as possible. If that's the case, building games as a hobby will start you on the path towards a new career in game development. Whatever happens, you're sure to learn something about yourself and gain some new skills along the way.

CHAPTER THREE
Salary and compensation

I'll always encourage you to follow your passion — but not if it's leading you into a life of poverty, ketchup soup for breakfast, and "retro" gaming because you can't afford a console from this decade. When choosing a career, you should also consider the more practical aspects of the job: Will it empower you in a healthy and enjoyable lifestyle? Could it support your current or future family? Can you afford to hit that big Steam sale with cash left over for pizza and Red Bull?

If I'm being honest with myself, I have to admit that I started my game career without giving much thought to the future. Testing games was hard work but it was fun, and I enjoyed working with other pop-culture geeks in the game studio. But as my paychecks flowed in and quickly out again, leaving me nothing extra to save for the future, it didn't take long to realize I needed a more lucrative job if I was ever going to upgrade my car or buy a house someday.

Early in your career, you may be exploring a variety of interests. Should you be a game designer, or a writer? Should you do character art, or environment art? Should you be a gameplay programmer, or an engine programmer? A producer, or a product manager? As you follow your interests and grow your skills, it's smart to take your future salary potential into consideration. This chapter will help you understand which game jobs pay the most (and which ones come up short), and find out how to maximize your income throughout your career.

Which video game jobs pay the most?

In general, game programming jobs pay the most. They start around USD

$40,000 per year and can easily reach over $100,000 after six years of experience. And that's even if you don't pursue a leadership role — most of the other game jobs only offer over $100,000 salary if you lead a team, but programmers can make that much as individual contributors.

Game art jobs have the widest variance in pay, depending on the type of art being done. Some entry-level artists can get around $35,000 per year, but others, such as 2D artists, can start as high as $60,000. Artists can make upwards of $80,000 after six years of experience, and over $110,000 for art leads or art director roles.

Entry-level salary for game designers is $40,000 per year, and it tops out around $100,000 for very senior designers, or for designers who play a lead role on game projects.

Game testing, unfortunately, has the lowest average pay of all the game jobs. Entry-level game testers can start as low as $38,000 per year, and sometimes even lower for hourly workers or contract workers. The maximum testing salaries can top out around $60,000, and that's only if you become a team leader or run a small QA group.

Salary is an important consideration when you're planning your career, but also consider what makes you happy. Pulling in the biggest possible paycheck might not be worth spending your life doing something you hate — or, worse, spending your life not doing something you love.

Why is there such a big difference in pay between jobs?

There are dozens of different jobs in the game industry, and each one of them has a different pay range. That's partly because each job contributes a different amount of value to the game company, but it's also due to simple supply and demand: if there's a shortage of people who can do a certain job in a local region or in the game industry as a whole, then those jobs will almost certainly pay more — and vice versa.

For example, game programmers are generally paid the most of anybody on a game team, where salaries can be as high as $250,000 a year for a technical director job. Technical Director is a very senior job, but they're paid even more than people with similar years of experience in other jobs because there are fewer people who can do the job well (or, possibly, fewer people who are willing to do it for a lower salary).

On the other end of the spectrum from game programmers are the game testers. Testers are often paid the least on a game team. Even a highly experienced game tester might have a salary cap of around $60,000 a year. That's a lot of money, but it's less than half of what a programmer would get paid for similar years of experience.

Programmers are paid more than testers because programming requires more education and training, meaning that there are fewer programmers in the world compared to testers. In other words, there's a lower supply of programmers compared to testers, so the laws of supply and demand drive programmer salaries much higher. With such a large difference in salary between the various game jobs, it's an important factor to consider in your career decision.

Why do entry-level jobs pay so much less?

The short answer is because entry-level developers aren't just lacking in key knowledge — they don't even know what they don't know. Game development is a big, deep, complex job, so it can take several years of on-the-job experience before you'll be highly valued by a game company.

But as you get more experience, you'll learn more skills. You'll be able to accomplish more work faster, and you'll make better decisions each day you work on a game project. You'll make a lot of mistakes and, hopefully, you'll learn from them so you'll be less likely to make the same ones again in the future.

All of that expertise will make you a faster and more reliable game developer, and that will translate directly into a higher salary year after year. As an example of how all that experience might affect your pay, let's look at game designers. Game designers with fewer than three years of experience are usually paid around $53,000 a year, but designers with over six years of experience can make as much as $80,000 per year. That's a big difference in pay, and it's all because employers value that experience and are willing to pay a premium for it.

Do game companies offer bonus pay?

A bonus is a lump sum of additional cash, on top of your normal salary, that a game company may pay you if your game sells well and makes a lot of money. If your game does exceptionally well, you could earn bonuses that add up to as much as 50% extra on top of your normal salary.

Unfortunately, not all game studios offer bonuses to their employees. And even when they do, it's never guaranteed — if your company doesn't make enough money in a given year, then they're unlikely to pay any bonuses.

The problem is, as a game developer, you don't always have direct control over your company's profitability. For example, several of my friends work at a game studio that's been giving big bonuses over the past few years. But this year, even though my friends' game was quite profitable, the company as a whole missed their revenue targets and the CEO has frozen bonuses across the entire company.

When you receive a job offer, be sure to find out whether they offer bonuses so you can compare that with other job offers you may also receive.

- If the job includes bonuses, look over the specific terms to make sure the goals they're setting seem attainable under normal circumstances.
- Ask whether the company has given bonuses in previous years. If they've never given a bonus, then don't factor that into your decision, since there's little evidence that you'd ever receive one.

Bonuses are nice when they're available, but don't count on them as a sure thing — because it's income that could vanish at any time without notice. Instead, think of bonuses purely as icing on the salary cake.

How can I find out what salary I should ask for?

When you apply for a job, it's common for the company to ask, "What are your salary requirements?" If this throws you for a loop, you're not alone. It's a hard question to answer — you don't want to ask for a huge number and scare them off, but you also don't want to work for peanuts and feel like a sucker.

The solution is this: ask for a competitive salary range for your job type, but also let them know that it's negotiable. That solves both problems — you've asked for a salary that reflects your worth, but you've also shown that you're flexible.

How do you know what salary is reasonable to ask for? Start by researching online to find out what salary range is competitive for your job type, based on what others are being paid to do similar jobs at similar companies in the region.

One website that's great for salary research is GlassDoor.com, which offers searchable salary data submitted anonymously by employees at various companies. You can get a sense of what range you should ask for by searching for salaries by job title, region, or even by specific company. Note that most game jobs go by different names at different companies, so be sure to try similar searches. For example, a programmer should try "programmer", "engineer", "developer", "game programmer", and so on.

Another helpful website is Gamasutra.com, which does a salary survey of thousands of professional game developers each year. Their survey results are self-reported and, between you and me, I suspect some game developers over-report so they can take the higher survey results to their managers to ask for a raise when the results are published later in the year. In my experience, the salaries in the survey are 10-15% higher than what people in the industry actually make, but it's a good place to start.

You can also ask any of the people you know who are already in the game industry. Ask them what the people in your field are paid at their companies, or at other companies they've worked for. If you know people in your graduating class who have received job offers, they may also be willing to share their salary numbers with you. The more data you collect, the more confident you'll be when you get a job offer and start negotiating for a higher salary.

Is it okay to negotiate for a higher salary?

After you go through the interview process with an employer and receive a job offer (yay you!), the salary they offer you could be lower than what you expected. If this is your first job offer, you might be tempted to just take it — after all, shouldn't you be grateful that somebody is actually willing to hire you? Well, if you've done your research and you know the offer is lower than what others in your position are earning, then it's okay to ask for more before accepting the job.

Does the idea of asking for more money make you queasy? Rest assured that it's not considered impolite or greedy, it's a normal part of the job offer process. In fact, some employers offer less than they're actually willing to pay because they expect candidates to ask for more. And they'll probably give it to you, as long as it's reasonable. For entry-level positions in the game industry, you could get $3,000 to $5,000 more annual salary. But only if you ask!

Start by letting them know you're pleased about the offer and you'd like to discuss compensation in more detail. Here's an example email that you can customize to suit your needs: "Thank you for offering me the position of [position] at [company]. I'm excited about the possibility of working with such a talented group of developers! My research shows that an entry-level salary for this position is closer to [desired salary], so I would like to speak with you further about the salary you've offered. I'm certain that we can come to a mutual agreement. When would be a good time for a phone call to discuss further?"

Be polite but firm. If you've done your salary research, then feel confident that what you're asking for is reasonable. Remember, the company obviously thinks you're something special, otherwise they wouldn't have offered you the job. If they agree, then they'll send you a new offer letter with the new, higher salary number. (Yay, you!)

Not all employers are willing to negotiate — they might say that the offer is final. If so, you'll have to decide whether you want to take it, or thank them for their time and continue your job search. My advice is this: If the salary is near your target range, and if you like the company and think it will be a great job, then go ahead and take the original offer. Otherwise, keep looking! There are plenty of jobs out there, so keep looking until you find a company you love and will pay you what you're worth.

CHAPTER FOUR
Getting a formal education

Not long ago, I took a road trip to a tiny town in Washington state, to attend my twenty-year high school class reunion (go Bulldogs). I graduated in 1992, way before social media was invented, so a couple of decades had gone by since I'd been in touch with most of my classmates.

Besides the shock of seeing that all the "cool kids" were now bald and had sizable beer bellies, I was also struck by the apparently wide range of income levels among my classmates. As the weekend went on and we chatted about lives, families, and careers, a pattern seemed to emerge: there was a clear divide between those who continued to college or university after graduation, and those who did not.

Granted, this was not a scientific assessment; it was based purely on anecdotal conversations. Some of my classmates had obtained a degree, moved to a city, and now have comfortable lives, while others stayed in town, got an entry-level job at a local business and, now quickly nearing their fortieth birthdays, they were struggling to stay afloat financially.

Getting a degree is not a guaranteed formula for success. I know people who got a degree but ended up hating their field, and I know people who didn't get a degree but are successful anyway. But there's a lot more than just anecdotal evidence in favor of post-secondary education: my high school reunion observation of a strong "return on investment" from a college degree is supported by numerous studies across many industries. College is a popular path after graduation, and for good reason.

How much education is enough, and what types of schooling are helpful in the game industry? And is it possible to get into games with no schooling at all? The answer is anything but straightforward. This chapter dives in to answer these questions and more.

How much education do I need for a company to hire me?

New employees come into the game industry through many different paths. Some have a formal education, some come from completely different industries, and some have no professional experience at all. So you don't necessarily need any formal schooling to get a game job.

However, getting a degree or certificate from a college or university, especially a game-specific degree, can often get you hired sooner, and at a higher starting salary.

Why is that? It's because employees who come through video game schools have proven that they've learned at least the basic skills, they already have some game development experience, and they usually have a portfolio of game demos that they've made as school projects. All of that tangible evidence that you can do the work of game development gives employers confidence in your abilities, and it can make them more willing to pay you a higher starting salary. A game school education may not be a requirement, but it's a proven way to get experience and build a portfolio to help you start your career on the right foot.

What education is required to get a job in game development?

The education requirements are different for each job family, and every game company has different requirements as well. The best way to find out what's required for a specific job you're interested in is to find a job posting online, and see what they list in the Requirements section. But here's a brief overview of the requirements you'll see most often.

Most programming jobs will ask for a bachelor's degree in a field like computer science, or a related field that emphasizes computer programming. There are also specialized schools that offer degrees in game programming specifically, or in "real-time" interactive systems or simulations.

The education requirement for game designers isn't very standardized. Game designers can come from a variety of backgrounds, ranging from computer science, to art, to media or the humanities. But many designer job postings will mention that they want you to have a bachelor's degree in something (anything!), even though it's not always a hard requirement.

Most game art jobs will also ask for a bachelor's degree from an art-related field of study. Many colleges and universities actually offer video game-related art degrees, which is great. Others offer degrees with a focus on video games or interactive media, as part of their traditional art degrees. Any of those could be a solid way to start a career in game art.

Game testing jobs don't usually require any formal education, but that's part of the reason the pay is lower than the other game jobs — the education requirements are also lower, so it's much easier to get a testing job if you don't have a formal college or university degree.

Could I get hired if I take an online game course?

In the past, online courses were the stuff of late-night infomercials and laughable TV spots about "tightening up the graphics on level 3" (google it). Fortunately, online degrees have come a long way. If you're looking to change your career, taking game development courses in the evenings and on weekends is a great way to start.

Quite a number of community colleges have started offering game design and game development courses, so check the local community colleges near you to see if they offer game development as part of their adult continuing education programs. You'll learn game development quickly, and you'll start making connections with other game developers and instructors that could help you get a job after you graduate the program.

I can personally vouch for the effectiveness of this option, because it's how I made the transition from my job as a game tester to my first job as a designer and programmer. The year-long certificate course from the University of Washington burned up my weeknights and weekends for a full year, but it was one of the best decisions I've made for my career.

What high school classes will prepare me for game design?

Most high schools don't teach game design. But take heart: game design is a multi-disciplinary career, meaning that you'll be best prepared for a job if you also learn skills used by other jobs on a game team. Not only because it will help you work more effectively with a team, but also so you can do some of the work yourself whenever necessary. So if you're in school, one way to start on the path to game design is to take classes that teach you the skills used by all jobs on a game team.

Start by taking some programming classes, because most game engines require you to use a simplified version of a programming language — often called a "scripting language" — to define the various ways the player can interact with a game world. For example, if you want a secret door to open when the player steps on a pressure plate, you could make that happen by writing code in the game engine's scripting language. Learning programming will also help you work more effectively with programmers on your future game teams. Programmers translate your designs into code that powers the game, so understanding their work will help you communicate with them to code your designs exactly as you've envisioned.

I also recommend that you take some art classes. Learn the artistic basics such as composition, lighting, color, positive and negative space, and architecture. You'll need to use all of those things when you're constructing game levels. Art class will also help you practice drawing and sketching, and you'll learn how to explain your ideas in a visual way. Those skills will help you communicate your ideas to everybody on a game team — not just the artists — because, as humans, we all learn better in a visual way. When you pitch your ideas to your team, to a publisher, or to a game company, you'll be more successful if you can present your ideas visually.

You should also take some creative writing classes to learn the basic techniques of telling compelling stories. Sure, most people prefer games with great storylines. But as a game designer, you'll also use storytelling to pitch your ideas to your game team. It will help them understand your designs, understand what you want as a designer, and get inspired to build your vision. Not to mention, you'll be writing a ton of documentation, emails, presentations, and other day-to-day "business" writing, all of which will be a lot more fun if you can add a creative flair.

Game design is a multi-disciplinary job. You may be doing some programming, art, and creative writing on a daily basis, so taking those classes in school is a perfect way to start.

What's the best way to learn game programming in high school?

You can absolutely start learning game programming while you're in high school. There are three things you need to do: learn a programming language, learn a game engine, and then learn how to use the programming language inside of the game engine.

Learning a programming language might seem like a big first step. If you've never looked at computer code before, it might look weird and a little intimidating. But it's actually quite easy to get started — it's nowhere near as difficult as learning a new human language like Spanish or Chinese. Once you get started, you'll be able to write your first computer program in about ten minutes. (Most of us start with the modest but ever-popular "Hello World" program.) There are many game programming books and online courses that will help you learn quickly.

The second step is to learn how to use a game engine, which is a suite of pre-made software tools that help you make games faster. Examples of popular game engines include Unity 3D, Unreal Engine, and Amazon Lumberyard. Professional game developers use game engines to create massive, triple-A games, but beginners also use them to get up and running and making a new game right away. All the popular game engines offer online tutorials to help you learn.

The third step is to combine both of your new skills together, to start using your programming language inside of the game engine to program a custom game of your own creation. Most game engines have online tutorials to teach you how to do it, so you can visit their website and start exploring the tutorials on scripting. Just make sure that you've already done the other tutorials and have a firm understanding of the programming language and the game engine before you start on this third step.

Once you start programming inside of the engine, the sky is the limit. You can make just about any game. If you can imagine it, then you can probably build it with enough time and effort.

But each of those three steps is much easier said than done, especially since you can't spend all of your time working on it — you still have homework and other activities. It will take you many weeks of regular effort to get comfortable with your new skills, but it should be a lot of fun. (If it's not fun, then at least you've learned that game programming might not be a good career for you.)

Should I drop out of college and learn to make games on my own?

If you're considering dropping out of school, you've probably already asked this question of your family and friends. And they've probably all told you the same thing — that staying in school will help you get a better job, make more money, and have a better life.

I'm also going to tell you that, yes, most of those things about staying in school are likely to be true. But if you're still not convinced, it might be because that advice is somewhat vague. So let's dig deeper and talk about the specific, concrete reasons why staying in school is usually the best choice.

Reason 1: College makes you do things you don't want to do, and those experiences directly prepare you for the real world of game development. The real world doesn't care whether you like math — if your job requires you to work with 3D matrix transformations, then you'd better understand it whether you like it or not. Getting outside of your comfort zone is a good thing, and school often forces you to do it.

Reason 2: Game development is teamwork, and you don't learn teamwork by yourself. You can learn the basics of game art or game programming or whatever on your own, but solo study doesn't teach you how to work with a team, or how to step up and be a leader, or how to motivate a struggling teammate. Hiring managers in the game industry want proof that you can succeed as part of a team — that's why doing team projects in school is also great for your résumé.

Reason 3: College helps you build industry connections that you desperately need. One major way to break into the game industry is to already know people on the inside — people who can help you get a job at their company. But when you're new to the job market, you don't know anybody yet, so you don't have a professional network. When you attend a degree program, your classmates will form the seeds of your professional network and could play a critical role in helping you land your first job.

Reason 4: College coursework builds your portfolio and your résumé. As a hiring manager, one of the most important things I look for in entry-level applicants is a past record of what I called "GSD" — Getting Stuff Done. The best way for me to know whether an applicant can GSD is to look at their portfolio. College is full of assignments, which become portfolio pieces, which gives you a strong head start.

Do I need a college degree to become a video game tester?

In general, no. Testing is generally considered an entry-level position in the game industry, and most companies do not require their game testers to have college degrees. Many of the job postings for QA tester jobs online say that they'd prefer applicants with a degree, but that it's okay to have "equivalent experience" or a degree that's different from what they recommend.

What is equivalent experience, exactly, and what other degrees might be considered? I have several friends who work in game testing, so let's use them as examples. My friend Teresa is a game testing lead, and she went to school for a few years for nursing. My friend Bill got a Bachelor of Science degree in Administrative Management before he started his career as a game tester. My friend Keith has a Bachelor of Fine Arts in Industrial and Product Design. Teresa, Bill and Keith all have long, successful testing careers — all three of them became either lead testers or QA managers. Video game testers don't seem to have a common thread as far as their education. Many of them have degrees in various fields, but many do not. Personally, I started my own career as a video game tester and went on to do a variety of other game jobs, and I never did complete a four-year degree.

It's also common for people to work as testers to pay their way through college. I've known several who worked part-time while they went to school, or even worked full-time while they took "evening degree" classes after work and on the weekends. Then, after they got their degrees, they got a new job in the game studio doing what they went to school for — like art, programming or design. You can bet they got healthy pay increases to go with their career upgrades.

While a post-secondary degree isn't required, what is required is a love of gaming. You also need a variety of important "soft skills" like listening and communication, and you need to be self-motivated, detail-oriented, have a technical mind, and be a strong team player. You can read more about how to prepare for a job testing games by reading a copy of my book *Land a Job as a Video Game Tester*.

How can I find out what degree is required for the job I want?

College is expensive, especially if you don't end up working in the career you went to school for. That's why it's important to research online and figure out what education and other skills you'll need in order to get the job you want. There are two methods that you can use for finding out what education is required.

The first technique is using LinkedIn. You can search for the job on LinkedIn — for example, "game designer" — then click the "People" tab to view a list of people who have that job, and then view the profiles to see what they have listed under their "Education" section. I think you'll be surprised at how much the educational background varies between people in the game industry, because most game jobs don't have specific education requirements.

The second technique is to search for game job postings online, and then read the "Requirements" section to see if they mention any specifics. One way you can find game jobs is to go to GameIndustryCareerGuide.com, click on the "Game Jobs" tab, and then type your search (for example, "game programmer"). Again, I think you'll be surprised to find that the education requirements for most game jobs aren't very specific. It's common for jobs to require a bachelor's degree, but not any anything specific. Programming jobs often require a bachelor's degree in Computer Science, but most other jobs don't have such clear-cut requirements.

If you don't have a bachelor's degree and don't plan to get one, don't let the requirements scare you away — if you meet around 80% of the other requirements for the job, you'll still have a good shot at getting hired. Go ahead and apply anyway.

Would a computer science degree be helpful for a career in games?

A computer science degree will definitely open the door for you to become a game programmer, if that's what you're interested in. Game programming is a fun job (if you like programming!), and it's one of the highest-paying jobs in the gaming industry — game programmers sometimes make more than double the salary of other game jobs.

Aspiring game designers can also benefit from a computer science degree, because you'll often be required to do programming to create the game's levels, missions, and other player interactions. Some of the best game designers I know started out as programmers.

Besides those tangible benefits of a computer science degree, you can also think of it as an insurance policy: if you ever have trouble getting into the game industry, or if there aren't many jobs available in your area when you graduate, a computer science degree will help you get a job outside of games. You'll qualify for jobs in game-related industries like serious games, medical, or industrial or training or simulation, or you could apply for jobs writing business software, creating desktop applications or mobile applications, or working as a web developer.

In short, for a job as a game programmer or a game designer, having a computer science degree offers clear advantages. It will make it easier to get a job in games and other industries, and is likely to earn you a higher salary throughout your career.

Can I get a job testing games while I'm in school?

Most game testing jobs don't require a formal education, so why not earn a paycheck and get some on-the-job experience while you're working toward your degree?

That's almost exactly how I started my own career in game development. I got an entry-level job as a game tester, and completed a one-year game programming certificate course in the meantime. Not only did I earn a decent paycheck while going to school, but it also gave me the opportunity to make personal connections with people on the game development teams — people who helped me transfer to a different job inside the company after I'd learned my new skills and was ready to move into a new role.

I'll be straight with you, it was a lot of hard work. Holding down a full-time job while going to school isn't easy. But within just a few months of getting that certificate, I was able to get promoted into an entry-level programming job, because I'd shown the initiative to learn how to make games and I had plenty of code examples and game demos in my portfolio to prove it.

What education is required to become a video game designer?

Jobs in game design don't usually have specific educational requirements. Some designers go to a college that has a formal game design degree, while others get a degree in the arts or the humanities. Others don't have a degree at all, but are self-taught indie designers who made games on their own until their portfolio was impressive enough to get hired at a game company.

I examined this question recently by looking at the LinkedIn profiles of fifty-three professional game designers I've worked with over the years. I was quite surprised at what I found: about one quarter (23%) of the designers had gone to school for a game design degree, but around one in ten (9%) didn't appear to have a formal degree at all. The remainder had studied a wide variety of fields, including:

- 15% studied computer science — programming and other computer-related skills
- 17% studied the humanities — literature, English, Asian studies, and economics
- 13% studied art (which can be an important part of game design)
- 11% studied media — radio and television, video production, and similar fields
- 8% studied applied science — practical science-based fields such as engineering or electronics
- The rest had studied information technology or business

That's an unexpectedly large diversity of backgrounds for a group of people who all went on to have the same job title. But if there's one pattern that stands out from this informal survey, it's that most of those fields of study contain expertise that can be applied directly to game design: making assets such as code or art, communicating with a wide audience of game players, or crafting a story and understanding how people think about the world (virtual or otherwise).

The fact is, game design is a relatively new field of study. Video games as we know them today haven't been around very long, so there isn't a clear educational path to your first job like there is for jobs that have been around longer such as electrical engineering, finance, or surgery.

But that's a good thing, because it gives you options: if you're positive that you want to do game design, there are more colleges and universities than ever before that offer specialized game design courses. But if you aren't sure, then you have the flexibility to study something else that clicks with you, as long as you're building skills that could be used in a game design job later on.

How can I start my career in game audio?

Game audio engineering is a highly technical field, and you'll need to learn a variety of hardware, software, and production techniques before a game company will hire you. Most audio engineers learn the basics by taking online courses, or getting a related degree.

For example, Full Sail University in Florida offers two different bachelor's degrees, one in recording arts and the other in audio production. They also offer video game-specific courses, which makes it convenient to get experience doing game audio by collaborating with students who are making games in other departments.

But you can also learn the skills you need at many other trade schools or audio-specific schools around the country. It's not as important which specific school you attend — the most important thing is that you end up with a solid audio foundation, and you do a number of projects that will look great (sound great?) on your portfolio.

Attending an audio school will also kick start your professional career network. As your classmates graduate and get jobs all over the world, they'll become the beginning of your professional network — your eyes and ears inside of the game companies. They'll help you spot job openings, and even help you get interviews. Support from your network will be a key factor in landing a good job after you're done with your schooling.

Which university is best for a degree in video game design?

When you're choosing a college or a university, there are many things to take into consideration. And it's not just about how well the school is ranked for a particular subject area like game design — just because a school is top-ranked, that doesn't necessarily mean it's the right school for you. Choosing a university is a big decision that will affect the next several years of your life, so you should evaluate several schools in detail and try to make the best decision on at least these four criteria:

1. Will this school teach you what you need to learn? This is the easy one, just go to the school's website and see whether it has a degree program in the field you're interested in. If you aren't sure what exactly you'd need to learn to get a specific job, search the Internet to find job postings from video game companies hiring for the job you want, and see what they list as requirements.
2. Can you afford to attend this school? Getting a degree is expensive, and may take years of your life to pay off. If you can't afford a big name private school, that's okay — consider whether a less expensive local college might let you achieve your educational goals at a fraction of the price. Check out your options for financial aid, because nearly anybody can get grants or scholarships.
3. Will you like the school's culture and environment? If you're going to spend several years living at a school, you'd better make sure you'll like living there. How many students attend the school each year, and are the class sizes big or small? Is that a fit for your personality and how you like to learn? That's important. Find out where the school is located. Is it next to a rural town with lots of outdoor activities, or is it near a big party town with festivals and nightlife? You start by researching each school online, but there's no better way to explore a school's culture and environment than actually visiting the campus. Go during the week and just stroll around, or sign up for formal tours.
4. Are graduates from the school getting hired in the game industry? If most of a school's graduates are getting jobs, that's a strong indicator that it's a good school. Visit the school's website and

look for their "outcomes and disclosures" page, which is chock full of insightful data about the number of students in each degree program, the amount they spent on tuition, and the percentage that got jobs or internships after graduation.

If you think all that research sounds boring or hard, just remember that you're making a decision that will cost you or your family many thousands of dollars, and will impact the next several years of your life. It's worth the effort.

Do I need an art degree to get a job as a game artist?

What if you've been doing art for a long time, maybe taking courses online or at school, and you already have a high-quality portfolio? Could you get hired at a game company without spending any time or money on a formal art degree?

This is one of those questions that people in the industry argue about, so let's start by looking at some data. Did professional artists currently working in the game industry start their first jobs without having art degrees? To find out, I searched on LinkedIn for some of my friends who are game artists. What I discovered was that every one of them has listed an art education of some sort on their profile, but not necessarily a formal degree.

For example, I see Tim with an associate's degree in Computer Animation; Maxx studied film; Lisa got a bachelor's of Fine Art in Media and Animation; and Elaine has a bachelor's degree in Digital Arts. But others have a less traditional education, including Anthony, who has a certificate (not a degree) in 3D Design and Multimedia; and Eric, who does not have a degree but has taken several mentorship courses, including Animation Mentor, iAnimate.net, the Motivarti Mentorship program, and AnimSquad Animation. That's not a scientific sampling, but it's evidence that some type of structured education may influence your success as a game artist.

Besides, having formal education on your résumé can help you get an interview because it signals to hiring managers that you're serious about your career, and that you have drive, commitment, and follow-through. It also suggests that you've stretched your art skills in ways that self-taught artists might not have experienced, because art school makes you do all sorts of projects that you probably wouldn't have tried if you were learning on your own.

However — and this is important! — understand that going to art school does not *guarantee* that you'll become a talented artist. If you have natural talent and you've already worked hard on art by the time you start considering a formal education, art school can help you get to the next level. But there's a dirty little secret about art schools: they're businesses, and it's not good business to flunk out students who aren't talented. So even if you don't show talent in your coursework, the school may continue taking your money anyway. That's why, every year, art schools award degrees to hundreds or maybe thousands of graduates who aren't good enough to get hired as professional artists. They've got a tough road ahead of them as they struggle to get jobs with subpar art skills and a mountain of student debt.

But that's where the art portfolio comes in. If you have a strong portfolio, then an art director can look at it and immediately see whether you have the talent and range needed for the job. And it doesn't take an expensive art degree to build a strong portfolio. If you are talented and self-motivated, work hard on your art every day, leverage the online art resources and communities to critique your work, and constantly improve, then there's a chance that an art degree wouldn't be worth the time and expense.

CHAPTER FIVE
Learning on your own

There are some careers that frown upon people who are "self-taught." Most of us wouldn't be eager to fly on an airplane with a self-taught pilot, or to be defended in court by a self-taught trial lawyer. And I certainly wouldn't volunteer to go under the knife of a self-taught heart surgeon.

The game industry is different. We're not writing software to operate surgical lasers or military weaponry, right? We're just making entertainment software. The stakes are lower, which is why you're legally allowed to animate a 3D dragon or write the code for an epic boss battle, without getting a Ph.D. from an Ivy League university.

But that doesn't mean game development is easy, or that you can learn it in a weekend. Every type of game job requires a unique collection of skills and knowledge that's both broad and deep. You may be able to start in a weekend, but it will take decades of continued learning and practice to master.

Fortunately, you can learn much of it on your own using resources available on the Internet, mostly for free — that is, if you're adequately self-motivated and not afraid of a bit of hard work. But with such a vast collection of skills to learn, where do you start? How can you get traction right away, and build a sense of accomplishment that keeps you motivated? That's what this chapter is all about. Let's find out how to get self-started, how to grow your skills, and how to leverage your hobby work into a full-time job at a game studio.

How can I get experience making games on my own?

Making a game from scratch takes time and work, but there's a shortcut that will give you a feel for game development without starting completely from scratch: you can try your hand at "modding" (modifying) an existing game.

Most commercial games, especially the ones available for PC, come with level editors and other modding tools you can use to make new characters, new missions, new stories, or even entirely new game modes. Modding tools are often similar to what the game's designers used to make the game in the first place — in many cases, they're exactly the same. That's why, if you learn how to use modding tools, you're already on your way to learning the professional tools of game development.

Modding games is a great way to start experimenting with game design and understanding what makes a compelling game world, because you can show your mods to friends to get feedback. They'll tell you which parts of your mod are fun and which parts aren't fun — feedback that will help you understand, and begin to internalize, the subtleties of good game design. Modding experience will also look good on your résumé, and can give you a huge advantage when you start applying for game development jobs later on.

Which game engine should I use to make my first game?

As you know, video games can range in complexity from simple 1980s arcade-style 2D games, to massive and open-world 3D games. When you're ready to build a game of your own, choose a game engine that meets the needs of the game you have in mind, and also meets you at your current skill level and time constraints. Here are three game engines that you should consider, depending on your skill level and your game development goals.

If you haven't learned how to program yet, then check out a game engine called Stencyl (www.stencyl.com). It's a good choice for your first game because you don't need to write any code — just use the drag-and-drop interface to assemble pre-defined "blocks" of game logic to build your game world and creatures. There are hundreds of ready-to-use blocks, plus you can even download blocks that other Stencyl users have created and shared.

For 2D games that are a bit more advanced, I recommend GameMaker

Studio (www.yoyogames.com). This engine is sometimes used by professional game developers, but it's so easy to learn and use that even beginners will get up to speed quickly. Like Stencyl, GameMaker Studio offers drag-and-drop features to create game logic. But it also offers an optional scripting language called GML that's a great way to start learning programming, once you're ready. In fact, when I used to work at a mobile game studio, some of the designers used GameMaker to quickly prototype new game ideas — even though they didn't know how to do programming.

If you're making your first 3D game, I recommend starting with the Unity 3D game engine (www.unity3d.com). As a full-featured 3D game engine, it's beloved by indie developers and professional game studios alike because it's robust, easy to learn and prototype with, and can be used to build games for just about any platform from computers to mobile phones. Best of all, it's free for beginners, so you can download it today and get started.

These game engines may be easy to learn, but that doesn't mean it won't require plenty of time and effort to build a complete game. Each one has dozens of features you'll need to learn, so it requires time and patience. Luckily, most of them also provide excellent online tutorials to help you get up to speed. After you download and install any of the engines, just go to the website and you'll find plenty of tutorials to walk you through the process of making your very first game.

As with most things in life, the hardest part of making a game is just getting started. The best way to learn game development is to do it, so if you want to make games for a living someday, get started right now. Have fun!

What programming language should I learn first?

There are many different programming languages available, but the most common ones used for game programming are C++ (pronounced "see plus plus"), C# (pronounced "see sharp"), and Java. So which one should you learn?

The truth is, it really doesn't matter which one you learn first, because all programming languages work basically the same way. Even though each one has different keywords and language features, the most important thing is to learn the fundamentals of how any program language works. Those fundamentals — how to start thinking like a programmer, and how to use a programming language to construct a computer program — are nearly identical in all of the popular programming languages. So once you learn your first, it's relatively easy to learn any others you might need later on.

If you're not sure which language to pick, then let me pick one for you: I recommend you start with C#. Why? Because it's a strong modern programming language, and there are a huge number of books and tutorials available to help you learn. And also because it's the main programming language used to make games using Unity 3D, which is one of the most popular game engines currently available.

There are dozens of online resources that can help you learn C#, ranging from books to YouTube videos to in-depth paid courses on sites like Lynda.com. And if you get stuck, you can ask for help on any of the vibrant communities of coders helping coders, such as StackOverflow.com. If you have any interest in learning how to program, there's never been a better time to get started.

Can I learn how to be a game tester on my own?

Most companies don't require a college degree to be a game tester, but you will need some specific "soft skills" in order to succeed at a game testing job.

First of all, you need to be a gamer and love video games. Since you'll be spending hundreds of hours with whatever game you're testing, companies will expect that you already have some gaming skills and a gaming vocabulary. But since you're reading this book, I'll assume you already love video games and this requirement will be a slam dunk for you.

Next, you need to be a good communicator, because testers spend a lot of time communicating with their teams through email, chat, and in person. You should be able to listen carefully when others are speaking, ask questions to clarify what others are saying, and express your thoughts and ideas in a way that others can clearly understand. If your spelling and grammar aren't great, start working to improve that now.

A good tester also needs to be self-motivated and willing to take ownership of their work. Once you get the job, nobody is going to hover

over your desk to make sure you stay on task. There aren't any parents or teachers to hold you accountable — you'll be responsible for managing your own work and getting a lot done on your own, every day, even when nobody is telling you exactly what to do.

Another skill you'll need as a tester is to be very detail-oriented. Testers spend a lot of time looking for bugs, writing bug reports, verifying fixes, and regressing bugs that they had written previously. Succeeding at those tasks demands that you're observant, thorough, organized, and patient. A detail-oriented mindset is something you can learn and develop with practice, so start practicing now — you'll see yourself improve quickly once you start paying attention to it.

Lastly, a game tester needs to be technically-minded, because you'll be working with many types of hardware and software, and you'll often need to talk with technical people such as programmers and artists. Be curious, systematic, and analytical. Learn about the scientific method, and practice applying science-based thinking to your daily life at school and at home. Scientific thinking will help your testing career and many other aspects of your life. Learn how to do some technical things. If you can learn a little bit about the entire process of game development, like learning how to use a 3D art tool or learning how to do basic computer programming, that will help you become more technical over time. It's also a lot of fun, so there's a win for you and for your testing career.

By the way, all of these things are discussed in my book *Land a Job as a Video Game Tester*, in case you want a more in-depth discussion.

Could I become a video game translator if I know two languages?

Game translation is a booming industry. Any new video game can cost millions of dollars and take several years to create, so one way game publishers maximize revenue is by translating the game so it can be sold internationally. Most commercial games made by English-speaking developers are adapted for at least four other languages: French, Italian, German, and Spanish ("EFIGS"). Gaming is also exploding in China, Japan, South Korea, Brazil, and other large countries, so there's a demand for game translators who know those languages and cultures.

Translation is when you take a sentence in one language and write an equivalent phrase in another language (English "hello" becomes French "bonjour"). Most people who speak two languages can learn to translate between them quickly and efficiently, with a little practice.

But translation is only part of the challenge — games also need to be "localized." Localization is a bigger challenge, because it involves not only translating the sentences, but also taking into account the cultural differences between the source and target and regions. That's more complicated than simply speaking both languages, because it requires a deep cultural understanding that most people simply don't have. What are the cultural differences in how the game characters greet each other, argue, compliment, and interact socially? Which phrases are used by young characters differently than older characters? Which aspects of the game might not be allowed in a certain country, such as the depiction of blood, gore, or sexuality?

Another challenge of localization is the subtlety in language context. Humor, jokes, sarcasm, irony, and pop culture references usually can't be translated directly, so you need to understand the cultural subtleties and come up with a new, original equivalent. This cultural understanding is the hardest part, and may require you to spend time living in both countries before you can do it well.

That's why most of the game industry's translation work is outsourced to companies that specialize in game localization. If you're looking for a job as a translator or localizer, start by identifying and applying to localization companies. One of the companies I've used in the past is called Babel Media, which appears to have been acquired by a company called Keywords Studios (Keywordsstudios.com) with locations in Canada, Ireland, Italy, Singapore, USA, Japan, Barcelona, Shanghai and Pune. I'd suggest checking out their careers page as a starting point to your search. You could also search online for "video game localization" plus the name of your country, to find jobs near you.

Who comes up with the story for a game?

For starters, I can tell you where they *don't* come from: they don't come from some game-story guru in an ivory tower whose job is to dream up amazing ideas, and then dole them out to the lowly game developers to implement exactly as they're told. That's what many people think of when they imagine a job in game design, but it's a myth.

One way game developers find story ideas is by adapting proven commercial successes in books, movies, or graphic novels. Think about some of the most cherished books or movies of the past few decades: Star Wars, Harry Potter, Ghostbusters, The Nightmare Before Christmas — not to mention all the superhero books like Batman, Spider-Man, and the rest of the DC and Marvel universes. Those stories have been made into video games on every possible platform, precisely because they already have huge audiences that love the stories and are likely to buy the games.

Now, if you've played any of those movie-based games, you might have noticed that the quality isn't always high. Sometimes that's because characters and plot lines that make a good story in a linear medium like a book don't translate well into the non-linear medium of video games. Other times, it's because the companies who own the rights to make the games are more committed to making a quick buck than making a great game. But sometimes they do it right, and those well-loved characters and story are transformed into an excellent interactive gaming experience.

Not all games are based on existing stories. Many games are innovative and original, so you can't just build the game and write a story to sit on top of it — you have to start with the gameplay, and then weave a new story through it and around it, so that the story universe supports and enhances the game mechanics, and vice-versa. For example, a team of students at DigiPen Institute made a game demo as part of a student project, and it was so unique and innovative that part of the team was hired by a local game studio called Valve Corporation. As the game was developed further and the game mechanics were fleshed out, the writers at Valve created a story to weave through the game and explain the game's mechanics and goals to players while also revealing an original story universe. It was famously released as *Portal*, and if you've played it, you'll understand that the game wouldn't make sense without the story — and the story wouldn't make sense without the game.

What's the best laptop computer for game development?

I could tell you exactly which computer I would buy, but it might not be right for you if the tools you're using to build your game are different from mine. And it certainly wouldn't apply to people reading this book five years from now. Instead, let's talk about a decision-making framework you can use to find out what kind of computer you should buy now or in the future.

First, there's basic hardware you'll want in any laptop, such as built-in WiFi, USB ports, and Bluetooth. Luckily, most modern laptops come with them built in. But you'll want to pay special attention to the laptop's screen. Be sure to get a screen that's crisp, has good color, and is big enough to comfortably work on for several hours at a time, especially if you'll be coding or scripting. Even if you find a laptop with a screen that seems a little too big, and you think "There's no way I'll want to lug that beast around in my backpack," I'd still recommend a big screen if you can afford it — larger screens are less likely to cause eye fatigue after several hours looking at text and other tiny details as you work.

How much memory do you need? How much internal storage? How speedy of a processor? Which operating system? Not to mention, should you buy a Mac or a PC? Bear in mind that a computer is simply a collection of hardware that you'll use to run your game development software packages. To find out what hardware you need, start by deciding which software you're going to use, and then look on the software company's website to see a list of hardware they recommend.

There are several different programs you'll need to design and make your game: a web browser, a word processor like Microsoft Word or Evernote, a spreadsheet like Microsoft Excel, and a few others. But those smaller software packages will run on just about any computer, so they're not the ones you should be concerned about — the software you really need to pay attention to is the "game engine" software, which you'll use to create your game world and script the game. Most game engines are relatively complex and resource-intensive, so be sure to buy a computer that has enough power to run whichever game engine you plan to use for your game.

Fortunately, the companies that make game engines also publish recommendations telling you exactly what sort of computer you'll need. Go to the company's website and look for a page called "system requirements" to find a precise list. For example, right now if I look at the system requirements page for the Unity 3D game engine, I can see that my computer would need to have Windows 7 or higher if it's a Windows machine, and a graphics card with DirectX 9 capabilities, and so on. They helpfully mention that any computer made after 2004 should work. Or if I look at the system requirements for the Amazon Lumberyard game engine, it says that I'll need 8 gigabytes of RAM, 60 gigabytes of disk space, and so on. All of the minimum requirements are listed there on the company's website.

But keep in mind, the minimum requirements listed on those pages are just that: a minimum. If you can, it's always better to spend a little extra money for a computer that exceeds the minimum requirements. That will make the game engine tools run even better on your computer, and you'll be able to keep the computer longer before you have to replace it and buy a new one in a few years.

So that's how to figure out which computer you should buy. Choose which game engine you'll be using, look for that game engine's system requirements, and then buy a computer that meets or, preferably, exceeds the requirements.

How did you start your own game career?

I started my career as a game tester at a studio called KnowWonder, in Kirkland, Washington. We made kids' games for PC and Mac, and one of my first projects was Harry Potter and the Chamber of Secrets. It was built on the Unreal Engine, and I think it was the first ever 3D adventure game for kids (although I know a ton of adults who loved it too).

That was my first "game" job, but I started learning about interactive software development a few years earlier when some friends and I started a little software company in our spare time. We had full-time jobs selling computers at a retail store, so we built our first product, Virtual Seattle, in our evenings and weekends. That's when I learned how to do 3D art, and when I taught myself how to do programming so I could create tools to help make more art in less time.

That's also when I learned how to work hard, fast, and smart. When you only have a few hours a week to build your product, it teaches you to focus on the job immediately at hand, and to create clever solutions to achieve your goals when you don't have time to do it "the right way." It also taught me the value of being a jack-of-all-trades. Those skills certainly came in handy for game development.

CHAPTER SIX
Applying for jobs and internships

I have a friend who absolutely despises the process of finding a new job. The very thought makes his nose wrinkle. He hates the search, he hates filling out online applications, and he *really* hates what he once referred to as "those awful interview questions."

The funny thing is, he's an extremely experienced gameplay programmer and has been writing code for big-name projects since 1997! With over twenty years experience, dozens of games to his name, and a stellar résumé and portfolio, why on Earth does he have so much animosity for the job hunt?

The short answer is, because job hunting can be time-consuming, frustrating, and sometimes a little demoralizing — even for a seasoned game industry veteran. There are dozens of game companies hiring right now, and hundreds of job openings. But, just like dating, it's all about finding the right match. Which of those job openings is the right fit for your unique combination of skills, talents, and personality? The process of finding out — searching, applying, and probably hearing "no" more often than "yes" — can be a blow to anyone's ego.

That's why your job search will go much smoother if you start by finding companies that are likely to be a good fit. Some people spray the Internet with job applications (I call it the "shotgun" approach to applying), but a better way is to be more targeted (the "sniper" approach) because it means you'll only apply to jobs at companies that you've already decided have a high likelihood of hiring you.

Start by reading this chapter to learn how to choose a company that's a good fit, how to "try before you buy" by doing an internship, and how to avoid being lured in by the many job websites that seem too good to be true (hint: they are).

What kinds of companies would be good to work for?

That's really up to you. What kinds of game companies do you like? Which games and genres are your favorites, or might be interesting to work on? Which game studios are in cities that you think you'd like to live in?

A good set of rules to help with a decision may include:

- Work at a company that makes games you're interested in. You'll be spending years of your life working on their games, and it will be more fun and engaging if you like what you're working on. You won't always get to work on games that you love to play, but it makes sense to do it whenever you can.
- Work at a company that's big enough to offer you various career options throughout your career. You probably won't want to stay in the same job forever, so try to work at a company that has several teams and several products, so you can have a chance to change teams, move up, or change your job role after a few years.
- Most importantly, work at a company that has friendly, fun, nice people working there. You may be working long hours for days or weeks leading up to big deadlines or releases. It will be much more enjoyable if the people you're working with aren't jerks. If you're lucky, you'll make some amazing lifelong friends.

How can I get my first job when companies require prior experience?

This is the classic chicken-and-egg problem that many people face when they're starting their careers. If you've recently graduated from college, or if you're trying to transition into a new career in games, how can you get hired if all the job openings require experience?

I've got some great news for you: It can be done! First, you need a strategy for getting just enough experience to convince a hiring manager that you're worth a shot. Then, once your foot is in the door, you're good to go. Because once you get that very first game job, you'll have professional experience on your résumé and your career is ready to take off.

One popular strategy is to do game art, design, or programming as a hobby, and then post your work in online forums (also called online groups or discussion boards). You might already read forums, and even leave comments and ask occasional questions. Professional game developers also use those forums, so it's a perfect way for you to get your work and your talent noticed by connections inside of game studios — maybe even hiring managers that decide who to interview and who to hire. That's how my friend Caleb got his start in the industry. He spent his time creating art and posting it to discussion boards like GameArtisans.org and Polycount.org and, eventually, somebody at a game studio noticed his work and offered him his first game job. So stop lurking, and start posting.

Another strategy is to build your own indie games. It might seem like a no-brainer, but there's no better way to get experience making games than to, well, make a game. My friend Dan got his start that way — he made his own indie games and posted them online. One day, people at a game studio noticed his work and offered him a job interview. There are several powerful and free game development tools available online, so there's no reason you shouldn't download one and start making your first game today. You're officially out of excuses.

In case you still aren't convinced that you can get hired without having "official" job experience, I'm going to let you in on a little secret: When a company lists their requirements on a job posting, most of the time they don't actually *require* everything on the list. There's always some flexibility. So use the "80-20" rule: if a job posting that says they want one or two years of experience, you should still apply if you can meet roughly 80% of the other requirements. Now you know.

What are the best job websites to post my résumé or CV?

When you post your résumé to a bunch of job boards, you probably get a nice feeling of accomplishment. Unfortunately, that feeling of accomplishment is about all you'll get, because posting to a job board is one of the least effective ways to get hired. And it doesn't matter if you submit it to one, or ten, or a hundred job boards, because chances are you'll never get contacted by an employer.

Résumés aren't for posting to job boards — they're for submitting as part of a job application. You start by finding a job opening that looks like it might be right for you, and then you apply to that job by filling out the online form and attaching your résumé.

How is applying for a job different from posting to a job board? Applying for a job is active, whereas posting your résumé is passive. When you post your résumé, you're basically saying, "Hey, employers, I'd like a job, any job. I don't even care who you are, just hire me please." You're rolling the dice and hoping somebody somewhere searches for your résumé and finds it. But when you apply for a job, you're actively telling an employer that you're a fit for their specific company and their specific job opening — it's like handing them your résumé and inviting them to interview you. That's a big difference.

So a better question would be, "What are the best websites for finding job openings I can apply to?" Here are some of my favorites.

- Indeed Jobs (Indeed.com). It's a job aggregator, so they crawl many different job posting sites and combine them all into one place. It's a big time saver.
- OrcaHQ.com is an excellent site that crawls the web pages of video game studios and publishers all across the world, and aggregates their job openings into one search engine on their website. It's really cool. I actually think it's just one guy who built it in his spare time, so if you find a job using his search engine, find him on Facebook and say thanks.
- GameJobHunter.com has been a game industry staple for years. It doesn't have a large number of job postings, but the ones they do have are current and high-quality. It seems to be especially good for jobs in game art, programming, design, or business jobs like marketing and production.

What is an internship, and is it worth the effort?

An internship is a special type of job you can only get if you're a student, and it's a great way to learn more about the game industry while you get on-the-job training and figure out which jobs to pursue after graduation. Most internships are for college or university students (though some accept high school students or non-students), and many colleges recommend that you do an internship as part of your coursework.

The hourly pay from most internships is low, and many "unpaid internships" don't pay anything at all. They're also temporary and short-term — usually just a few months or even a few weeks. So you're definitely not doing it purely for the money.

But internships offer a huge benefit to the game company, and an even bigger benefit to you, the student. Yes, the company gets an inexpensive worker to help out on a game project or a research project. But, more importantly, they get to test you out to see if you're somebody they'd like to hire full-time someday. Think of it as the company's "try before you buy" program for future employees. The benefit to you as a student is that you get on-the-job, real-world training. You also get the opportunity to start making connections inside of the game industry, which will come in very handy later on when you start to look for full-time jobs.

On top of all that, if you do a good job during your internship, there's a high likelihood that the company will offer you for a full-time job after you graduate. Even if you don't get hired by that company, the fact that you've completed an internship will give you an edge over all the other entry-level job seekers that don't have that same real-world experience. You'll have a clear advantage over the other applicants when you apply for game jobs after graduation. Well worth the effort.

How can I get an internship at a game studio?

Usually, only the biggest game companies — the ones with hundreds of employees around the world, like Nintendo, Microsoft, Electronic Arts, or Ubisoft — have enough resources to build and run formal internship programs. They typically post their open internship positions on job boards, so you can find them using a job search engine like Indeed.com, or you can check game industry job boards like Gamasutra.com or GameJobHunter.com. Or you can visit the corporate websites for game companies you're interested in, where they list their internship jobs and explain how their program works and how to apply.

What many people don't know is that smaller studios also accept internship applications from time to time. But since they don't have a formal program, you might need to be proactive and drive that process yourself. One way is to apply using the normal job application form on their website, but make a note on the form that you're looking for an internship. Hopefully they'll see your note when they review your application, and pass you over to whomever is handling their internships. If a game studio doesn't have an application form available on their website, you can try emailing or calling them directly to find out about their policies for internships.

Another approach that takes more effort but might work if the first two methods don't is to find out who the hiring managers are at the game studio, and then contact them directly. I have a super clever little trick to help you out with this — it's a bit devious but it can be really effective: Go to LinkedIn.com and search for managers by typing the name of the company into the search box, along with the phrase "human resources" or the word "director," plus the name of the applicable department. For example, if you want an internship at Bethesda Softworks, search for "Bethesda Softworks art director." That will run a search for all of the relevant directors at the company. Then, email them using LinkedIn and ask whether they have any opportunities for an intern in their department and, if so, how you can apply.

If LinkedIn doesn't allow you to email the director because they're not in your professional network on LinkedIn, you may need to upgrade to a paid account. It will cost a little bit of money, but it's worth it to get access to the hiring managers that could help you land an internship.

How can I make the most of my internship?

You might imagine that an internship is a formal, structured process — kind of like a class at a university, but at a game studio instead of a classroom. In most cases, that could not be farther from the truth. Often, the people that you'll be working with on the game team are too busy with their own jobs to spend much time teaching you in a structured way. To make the most of your internship, you should assume that it may be entirely up to you to drive your own success and learn as much as possible in the time you have.

If you were hoping for a more "directed learning" experience, then discovering that you might be on your own could be disheartening. But honestly, self-driven learning is a good skill to master because it's likely to be how you'll learn once you get your first full-time job. There's just not a lot of formal training at most video game studios. You've got to be able to take the work you're assigned, give it your best shot, and get comfortable with "bugging" your manager or your team leader whenever you have questions or get stuck.

Even though you're "just an intern," you'll still need to contribute something of value to the team — be sure to study and brush up on any game development skills that you might need to use on the job. And try to be somebody that they want to work with! Be friendly, positive, hard-working, and self-motivated. Especially self-motivated, because there might not be any managers with extra time to train you. Help them feel confident that you can learn well on your own, and can get work done without constant hand-holding.

Most of what you'll learn will come from the work that you're doing, the questions that you ask, the answers you get, and the opportunity to see the work and interactions of other professional game developers at the studio. It's not a "formal" education, but it's an excellent way to get advanced training while you also learn how to navigate a professional job as a game developer.

How can I find a job testing video games from home?

I hate to be the bearer of bad news, but work-from-home game testing jobs don't actually exist. Video game development is a team effort, and game companies want their teams to be together in one place so they can collaborate and communicate most effectively (and, honestly, to make sure that you're actually working instead of spending all day on Reddit).

But if you've ever searched the Internet for game testing jobs, you've probably seen websites claiming that yes, they can hook you up with a work-from-home testing job — for a price. Some will charge you a signup fee, while others require a monthly subscription. Some even have professionally-produced video testimonials of people who were "skeptical at first, but now I make $50,000 per year playing the hottest new games at home!"

Do those websites give you an icky feeling, as if they might be too good to be true? Congratulations, you were right — those sites are scams, created specifically to rip you off.

Game testing is a normal job, just like any other — you'll never (never never never) have to pay to apply. You can search for job openings on Internet job websites or directly on game company websites, then submit your job application and go through the interview process just like every other job on the planet.

Don't ever pay a website to help you get a job testing games. If you do, you'll end up without your money and without a job.

How can I tell if a game jobs website is a scam?

Unfortunately, many of the game job websites out there are scams, especially the sites for game tester jobs. So let's arm you with some mental tools for deciding whether to trust a website in case you find one you're not sure about.

Some scam websites are obvious. They use poor spelling and grammar, ugly graphic design, and scammy-sounding URLs. But not all of them are so easy to spot — some look awesome, with impressive visual design and professional-looking content. In those cases, you'll need to dig deeper to make sure.

First, look for hints that they might ask you for money to help you find jobs. Phrases like "Get access to game tester jobs," or "It does cost money to join our network" are suspicious because you should never (never!) need to pay to get access to jobs. Game companies want a large number of people to find and apply to their job postings, so they never hide them behind a paywall.

If you're still not sure, check the site's legal disclaimers, usually linked at the bottom of each page in small text. For example, one of the scam websites I've found in the past has a disclaimer that says "THERE IS NO GUARANTEE THAT YOU WILL EARN ANY MONEY USING THE TECHNIQUES AND IDEAS IN THESE MATERIALS." If the home page says "Get paid to play games" but the disclaimer page says "there is no guarantee that you'll earn any money," that's a big red flag. Stay away.

If you want to avoid these problems completely, you can apply for jobs directly on the corporate websites of well-known game companies, or stick to well-known job boards like Monster.com or Indeed.com.

Do game studios ever hire entry-level applicants?

Whether you've just graduated or you're switching careers, I'm sure you've asked yourself this question: Why would a company hire me when there are so many other applicants with game industry experience? Rest assured, hiring managers in the game industry do hire entry-level applicants, even without any professional experience. It's a common practice, and there are good reasons for it.

The first reason is your price tag. Employee salary is the single biggest expense for most companies, so hiring entry-level workers with lower salaries can help offset the high salaries of the experienced workers. Sometimes it's actually more cost-effective for a company to hire two entry-level artists, for example, rather than one experienced-but-expensive artist.

The second reason is your passion and enthusiasm. When I was a new game developer, I frequently worked overtime because I'd finally landed my dream job — I'm sure I wrote more code than more senior programmers on my team. Compare that intensity to somebody who's a lot more experienced, but has maybe become a bit jaded. Even though a ten-year industry veteran may be more skilled, veterans can get burned out and their productivity can decline. Sometimes the newbies are the real rock stars.

That leads to another reason why you may get hired over an industry veteran: You don't come with a heap of emotional baggage. As a hiring manager, I love it that new grads start with zero preconceptions about how they should work, how they should interact with a team, and how they should be managed. They're more open to trying new things, and they're less cranky when they don't get to do things their way.

The last reason is that entry-level workers are often more up-to-date on modern technologies and techniques. It's like that saying about teaching old dogs new tricks. It's true that a ten-year game dev veteran has more experience, but it's also been ten years since they were in school, and it may have been ten years since they worked outside their comfort zone to try something new. When a person has been doing the same job for a long time, it's common to get into a rut of doing things the same way they always have.

When you're applying and interviewing, be sure to show your passion, and that you're open to new ideas and eager to adapt to the company's ways of doing things. Build interest by talking about the cutting edge tools and techniques that you've been using at school — tools that your more senior competition looks at and says, "No thanks, I'd rather do things the old way."

What if I keep applying for jobs but I never hear back?

Do you imagine that game studios are "professional" companies with a rational, organized system for interviewing and hiring new employees? Bad news: the opposite is true. Many studios are small, disorganized, and under-staffed. If you've applied to a company that didn't respond to your job application, there are many reasons why it might have fallen through the cracks — and it may be up to you to give them a nudge to push the process forward.

First of all, crazy as it might sound, some companies might simply lose your application. It could be stuck in their applicant tracking system, or lost in somebody's mile-high email inbox. Even if your application has made it into the hands of a hiring manager, they might be overwhelmed with their "normal" work (programming, producing, etc.) and don't have time right now to consider your résumé. It's even possible that they've moved to a different position, or have left the company — and left your job application in limbo.

Or, it may be that the job you applied for is no longer needed. In the games business, things change quickly — teams get cut, and game projects get rebooted, redesigned, or canceled. Whenever a big change happens, management needs to rethink their staffing plan, and you might be left wondering why they didn't get back to you. If they do get back to you, it might be to tell you the job is no longer open.

What if they've seen your résumé or interviewed you, but then decided you're not a fit for the role? Normally, somebody at the company is supposed to call to let you know that they aren't moving forward with your application. But less experienced managers might drag their feet because, let's face it, it's no fun to be the bearer of bad news. Experienced managers are comfortable delivering this bummer of a message, but they might procrastinate if they're not good at handling conflict.

Are you surprised and a little frustrated at how often these professional-looking companies drop the ball in such unprofessional ways? You're not alone. It's one of the most complained-about aspects of any job hunt. The solution is to take the process into your own hands. Sometimes, all it takes to get the ball rolling again is a little push in the right direction. Here are some approaches for you to try:

- Contact the recruiter or hiring manager to ask if they can give you a status update. This could remind them that it's been a while since they've worked on their hiring responsibilities, and prompt them to move it forward.
- If you applied through an applicant tracking system, check to see if your status has changed (for example from "submitted" to "under review"). If not, then at least you know it's not a problem with your résumé – the ball has been dropped on their side.
- If you have a contact inside the company (as a result of your networking efforts — you've been networking, right?), ask them to talk with the hiring manager. See if they can get a status update for you.
- If the job was posted online, check the website to see if the job is still posted. If it's not, then the job opening has been closed or they've already filled the position by hiring someone else.

This dark cloud has a silver lining: If their process has stalled out on your application, it's probably also stalled out for the other people who applied for the same job. This is a chance for you to get ahead of your competition! Take the actions listed above to get your application moving forward again, while your competition sits around complaining that nobody got back to them.

CHAPTER SEVEN
Writing your résumé

Here you are, raptly absorbing every ounce of advice in this book, brimming with motivation to get a job in the game industry as soon as possible. At the same time, out there somewhere in the world is a hiring manager at a game studio who wants (needs!) to hire you, although she doesn't know it yet (that fool!). How can you find each other? And how can you convince the hiring manager that you're the perfect person for the job?

Writing your résumé (called a CV in some regions) is the first step of your job hunt, and it's an important document because it's your chance to tell hiring managers around the world who you are and what you can do. But a résumé shouldn't just summarize your skills and experience; it should also help you stand out from the dozens, maybe hundreds, of other people who are applying for the same jobs. A strong résumé makes a memorable first impression, and convinces the hiring manager that they want (need!) to contact you and schedule an interview right away — before they miss their chance and lose you to a different company.

Although the résumé is only your first step, it can sometimes be the most challenging. Do you struggle to figure out what to put in and what to leave out, or how to present your skills and experience in a way that's concise yet persuasive? Luckily, just getting started on your résumé is often the hardest part. Once you get going on it, there are a few simple techniques and rules you can keep in mind to create a résumé that's sure to get you an interview. Let's explore.

What's the best way to start writing my résumé?

When you start creating a new résumé, your first enemy is likely to be the blank page. You could spend hours researching different layouts, debating between chronological vs. functional, or obsessing over fonts and border styles. Rather than figuring it all out from scratch, it's best to skip the hassle and start with a résumé template. Just go online and search for "video game artist résumé" (or "programmer" or whatever applies to you), and you'll find hundreds of passable résumé templates to use as a starting point for your own.

Another way to get a template is to use one of the built-in templates inside whatever word processing software you're using on your computer. Whether you're using Microsoft Word, Pages by Apple, or even Google Docs, they all have built-in résumé templates that you can choose from. Choose one that looks clean and professional, but don't spend time scrutinizing the differences — just pick a template and then get started writing.

Should I include a summary statement or an objective?

A résumé's summary statement is a two- or three-sentence paragraph that gives readers an introduction, or an overview, of what you have to offer a company as a potential employee. Some hiring managers like to see summaries on the résumés they receive, and some don't care — it just depends on their personal preferences. But I think adding a summary is a best practice, because it gives the reader context and piques their interest in reading the rest of your résumé.

It's hard to explain what a summary should look like, so here are a few examples to illustrate. The summary for a game tester résumé might look like this: "Enthusiastic, self-motivated, and detail-oriented software tester, with experience in console and mobile games." See how just a single sentence can offer a strong overview of who you are and what you can do? Another example, this time for a game programmer, might look like this: "Computer science graduate and lifelong gamer geek with experience building a mobile indie game from the ground up." Again, that's only a single sentence, but it conveys several things: education, specific experience, and passion for the game industry. Obviously, your summary should be specific to you, so look at other people's summaries to get ideas but don't copy them exactly. Write yours to be specifically tailored to your own skills, background, passions, and personality.

Now, some people will tell you to write an "objective statement" at the top of your résumé instead of a summary. I do not advise that. What's the difference? An objective statement says what you want to *get from* a company, whereas a summary statement says what you can *give to* a company. A hiring manager trying to fill a job opening doesn't care what you want — she cares about what you can do to help her game team succeed. That's the goal of your summary statement.

How can I write a résumé that stands out?

The meat of any résumé is the list of jobs you've had, called the "experience" section. For each job you list in this section, you should include your job title, the dates you worked there, and a list of the key responsibilities you had at the job. Most people stop there, but that's a mistake! If you only include a simple list of job responsibilities, you're missing the opportunity to tell about your job accomplishments. Many résumés do not list their accomplishments, so this is a chance to stand out from the crowd.

When a hiring manager is reading your résumé to find out whether you might be a fit for her job opening, the key question in her mind is "can this person accomplish the job." A list of your past jobs and responsibilities tells her what you've been assigned to do in the past, but it doesn't show evidence that you were any good at it. So it's important to list your major accomplishments, because it helps hiring managers understand how you've succeeded in the past, and gives them confidence that you'll continue to succeed in the future.

So for each job you list on your résumé, also include three to five bullet points that clearly state what you accomplished at the job, and why that accomplishment was important to the company. Be specific, and use numbers whenever possible. For example, instead of writing "optimized the frame rate of the game," you could be more specific and include numbers such as "optimized the game's frame rate, increased from 45 frames per second to 60 frames per second." That's a powerful and attention-grabbing way to highlight your accomplishments. Instead of writing "part-time artist for indie game Crazy Caverns," you could include specific numbers such as "part-time artist for indie game Crazy Caverns, created 16 low-poly animated characters and 450 unique environment props." Isn't that more impressive? That's the power of being specific.

Be specific about what you've accomplished, and I guarantee your résumé will put you ahead of the pack.

Should I optimize my résumé to be searched by bots?

In the old days, back before anybody had heard of "Y2K" or "xkcd," recruiters and hiring managers had to do the hard work of sifting through hundreds of résumés looking for the right candidates to bring in for an interview — and they had to do it manually. These days, many companies use software called ATS (applicant tracking systems) to automatically bulk-filter thousands of résumés by matching them against certain keywords that pertain to the job.

In other words, robots are reading your résumé.

ATS software is used by many large companies, and large game companies are no exception. But that doesn't mean the process is completely automated, or that you won't have a chance for your résumé to be read by humans. Sure, if you truly don't have the required skills or experience, then the software might reject your application automatically. But, in that case, a human would have rejected it as well. If you're close to being qualified, then the software will send your résumé to be personally reviewed by the recruiter or the manager in charge of hiring. If the robot passes your résumé and the humans believe you might be a good fit for the job, then they'll call you in for an interview.

It's impossible to know exactly how to optimize for the ATS software, because it's a moving target — each one is different, and the algorithms tend to evolve each year. And the algorithms are smart, so they won't fall for simple tricks like keyword stuffing. So instead of trying to game or manipulate an unknown automated system, it's best to just write a good résumé for humans. Be sure to mention all of your relevant skills, education, and background, and the ATS will find it.

In short, write your résumé to be read by humans, and don't worry — the robot overlords will pass it along to the right people.

How can I write a good résumé if I'm not a good writer?

So you've been working on your résumé for days. You've started with a good template, added a strong summary statement, and filled in the key details about your past jobs and accomplishments. Finished, right?

Not quite. The last step, and one of the most important, is to make sure there isn't a single spelling or grammar mistake. Not even one! The problem is, you're no longer an objective reader because you've been staring at it for too long. So for this last step, you need to get somebody (or several somebodies) to proofread it for you, and give you suggestions on spelling, grammar, and other content and structural improvements.

Why is proofreading so important? Because if a hiring manager finds typos or grammar mistakes on your résumé, it hints that you might be a sloppy worker who doesn't pay attention to detail. As a hiring manager myself, I'm super picky about any mistakes on the résumés I read. (I'd better make sure there aren't any mistakes in this book, or I'll get a raft of indignant e-mail from readers!) And I know other hiring managers who are much stricter than me — they'll immediately throw away any résumé that contains a spelling error. That's why you need to make sure it's perfect.

Ask several people to proofread your résumé. Choose from anyone you know who would be open to helping you out — friends, parents, coworkers, even teachers or professors at your school. Any of them may have good ideas for improving your résumé. Besides checking the grammar and spelling, you can also ask for their opinions on skills and abilities they might see in you but you don't recognize in yourself. Consider working that feedback into your résumé as well.

If you get suggestions and improvements from several people but you still think your résumé needs more work, consider hiring a professional résumé writer. If you search for professional résumé writers online, you'll find there are thousands to choose from. But it's difficult to tell which ones are any good, so try to get a recommendation from somebody you trust, such as a guidance counselor or career counselor. In a pinch, freelancer websites such as Fiverr.com and UpWork.com are full of résumé freelancers — but before you hire anybody, make sure they've received plenty of positive reviews from past customers.

CHAPTER EIGHT
Building your portfolio

When you apply for your first job at any game studio, your biggest challenge is to prove to them that you've got the right skills for the job — even though you've never actually shipped a commercial video game. If the hiring managers who read your résumé aren't convinced, then they won't call you in for an interview, and you won't have a shot at getting the job. There's a lot on the line.

So how do you prove you can do the work, if you don't have any professional experience? That's where your portfolio comes to the rescue. When you link to it from your job application, it shows the hiring manager some of your best work and gives her enough confidence to contact you for an interview. That's why having a strong portfolio is critical to a successful job search. Whether you're an artist, programmer, designer, audio engineer, or anything else, building a great online portfolio should be a top priority.

If I have a degree, why do I need a portfolio?

For many graduating students, their biggest fear is not being able to get a job. Not only are you competing for jobs with established industry insiders, you're also competing against your entire graduating class. And guess what? There probably won't be enough jobs for everybody. If you don't stand out from the crowd, you'll be left behind.

I've been a hiring manager for years, and one of the biggest challenges for any hiring manager is assessing whether or not an applicant could actually deliver great results on the job. I look for candidates who have a strong résumé and cover letter, of course, but that's only your first hurdle — you still need to successfully pass one or more interviews, and possibly even a "take home" test. But hiring managers know that interviews can be misleading, and even tests aren't foolproof because they can be gamed by dishonest candidates.

The only guaranteed way for hiring managers to know whether a candidate can deliver great future results is by evaluating their past results. Do you have a history of creating great work? Maybe you do, but you still have to prove it to me. If you're a level designer, show me a portfolio containing some clever and interesting levels you've built. If you're an artist, your portfolio should have a video showcasing your concepts, models, effects, and animations. If you're a programmer, I'd like to see interactive versions of your coursework such as AI pathfinding or rendering effects, along with your source code.

What's even better? Since you're applying for a job making video games, there's one surefire way to stand out and prove that you can deliver: show me a playable video game demo that you worked on. It's hard to argue with actual results. I'm shocked at how few candidates bother to send me a demo of good work they've done at school or in their free time at home.

What if your portfolio doesn't contain an interactive demo of your work? Then you'd better get to work building one. Because I can guarantee, at this very moment, somebody else from your graduating class is building a sweet little demo right now. And they're about to get that job instead of you.

How can I tell whether my art portfolio is good enough?

There's only one way to know for sure: you need to receive candid, honest feedback from people who have the right experience to evaluate your portfolio from a professional standpoint.

One way is to reach out to artists and art directors in the game industry, and ask them for feedback. Game artists are a tight-knit community, so it should be easy to find artists who'd like to help you with a portfolio review. (Other people helped them out when they were first getting started, so they want to pay it forward to the next generation.) You can also post your portfolio link to any of the online art communities and ask them for feedback. You won't always get detailed advice, and you may need to read between the lines to hear what they're really saying about your portfolio overall, but you're sure to get some tactical tips you can apply to your portfolio's content, structure and presentation.

If you think your portfolio is already in decent shape and you don't mind being bold, you can take a more direct route and start applying to game art jobs now. If the companies you apply to don't call you back, or if you get interviews but you don't get job offers, try asking the company's art director why she didn't pick you. If it's because your portfolio needs work, ask her for specific and usable feedback that you can apply to improve your portfolio for the future.

There's one place you should *avoid* going for feedback, and that's your friends and family (unless they're professional artists themselves). People who are very close to you are unlikely to be objective, so they're unable to be candid with you about your artwork. In fact, they're likely to tell you exactly what you want to hear: that you and your art are awesome. They can't be trusted! Instead, go to more experienced artists and tell them you only want the hard truth and nothing but the truth, even if it stings. Then swallow your ego, take all that feedback to heart, and get to work on improving that portfolio.

Do programmers need an online portfolio?

An online programming portfolio is simply a personal website containing examples of your game programming work. It shows what you did, and why you did it that way. There aren't any established standards for what it should look like or what exactly should be in it, so you don't need to match any particular layout or format. It just needs to give hiring managers a favorable impression of your work.

A good approach to showing and explaining your work is to include what I call "the What, the Why, and the How" of each of your game programming examples.

To show the "what" of your work, show the visual output of your demos — for example, an executable demo that a hiring manager can run in her web browser on her work computer. Another approach is to create a video of your demo, in case the hiring manager can't run it or doesn't have time to download it. Hiring managers are busy people, so you'll score points by making it as fast and easy as possible for them to view your work. Artists often make what they call a "demo reel," which is a short video montage that showcases footage from all of their best work. That's also a good idea for your programming portfolio because it offers a quick, high-level overview. But you'll still want to do individual videos for each of the demos in your portfolio to give hiring managers an in-depth look.

Next, to show the "why" of your work, include a short paragraph to explain what your sample is trying to demonstrate; what you intended to learn by creating it; and what challenges you encountered, and then overcame, during development. The explainer paragraph puts your game demo in context and shows that you're a thoughtful, curious programmer who loves a challenge. And it highlights the fact that you've learned something valuable along the way.

Lastly, show the "how" of your work. Since you're a programmer, the "how" is almost always your source code. No matter how great your demos look, it's important that you've written good code — the hiring manager will definitely want to see it. You can let the hiring manager download a ZIP file, or you can include the most relevant sections right in the web browser, or you can provide a link to your source code in an online repository such as GitHub. It's up to you, as long as the hiring manager gets to see your code.

Put it all together and you've got a programming portfolio. I've read through job applications from literally hundreds of programmers, and very few of them had an online programming portfolio. The ones who did really stood out from the crowd. It's a great way to catch the attention of hiring managers and pique their interest enough to call you for an interview.

What types of demos should I have in my programming portfolio?

Most any programming project could go into your programming portfolio, but the more visual the better. If you're taking programming courses in school, then you're likely to have assignments you could include, but if not, then consider making a small game using a game engine like Unity 3D or GameMaker. If you haven't made a demo yet, then I recommend you get started right away.

But what to make? There are several kinds of programming jobs in the game industry, so the demos you make for your portfolio should be applicable to the type of job you're working toward.

Graphics programmers work with shaders and rendering effects, so make a few demos that showcase your knowledge of the rendering hardware and pipeline. For example, my friend Brandon is a graphics programmer, and his portfolio includes interactive demos of procedural GPU shaders he wrote using GLSL (a shader language). He hosts them on GLSLsandbox.com, where hiring managers can see his source code and watch his special effects in action. You might also enjoy implementing an algorithm from any of the graphics technology research papers that are released at the SIGGRAPH conference each year — just search online for "SIGGRAPH technical papers" and you'll find plenty of interesting, portfolio-worthy challenges.

Tools programmers write software that helps their team's artists, designers, and other developers do their jobs faster or easier (or both). They often code their tools inside of other content creation packages such as Photoshop or Maya, so a nice portfolio piece would be to write a plugin for one of those programs. For example, write a plugin that allows artists to add game-specific data to a character model, and then exports the data for later use by a game engine. Or you could write a plugin for a game engine editor like Unity 3D or Amazon Lumberyard. Remember that you'll be showing it to potential employers, so be sure your code is clean and well-organized.

Game programmers write the code for player movement, enemy intelligence, weapons fire, and other systems related to game rules and gameplay. For a game programmer portfolio, there's nothing better than making an actual game that a hiring manager can play. It's always impressive (and fun!) to choose a simple game from the early arcade era such as Space Invaders, Asteroids, or Pac-Man, and then re-create it from scratch. If possible, make your game work inside a web browser so hiring managers can play it without downloading and installing.

Those are just a few ideas. But really, any demo that shows your passion for programming and game technology will do. The best portfolios I've seen have a variety of technology such as rendering, physics, pathfinding, and playable game demos. I can play the demos to see if the coder has a good feel for player interaction, and I can view the source code to see how well she architects and organizes her code. When there's a variety of project types, it indicates that the programmer is passionate about coding, and that she's curious and motivated — in short, she'd be a great hire.

What should I put into my online art portfolio?

Building an online portfolio is an absolute necessity for landing a job making game art. But there's more to it than simply showing your awesome work to the art director before an interview — it's also important to highlight your individual passion and personality as an artist. So showcase your art with a personal flair, and don't be afraid to let your unique personality show through.

Since I'm not an artist myself, I asked some of my art lead and art director friends to offer their best advice on building a strong online art portfolio. So here it is, a rapid-fire list of insights from creative leaders who know how to make an art portfolio that demands attention.

- Only show your professional-level work if you expect to be paid to do a professional-level job. Even one bad-looking image will detract from the whole, and sometimes that's all it takes to remove you from consideration. It's better to include ten images that rock than a hundred that make your work quality look inconsistent.
- Set up your portfolio site with tabs to demonstrate multiple skill sets, because being diverse in the game industry is valuable. As art directors review animators' portfolios, they often look for artists who can wear multiple hats. Try to show as many styles and ideas as you can.
- Navigation should be clear and easy. The fewer clicks it takes before your gallery is presented, the better.
- Don't distract from the work. Focus your presentation around the images, not the interface.
- Always push yourself, and get critique and feedback from the most critical person you know. If you apply for a job and get rejected, ask for feedback and take it seriously.
- Make it easy to find you. Your contact info should be easily accessible from any point on your site.

- Looking professional doesn't mean you have to spend all your time and effort creating a website if you could be making new art instead. Find a way of uploading your work that meets your needs and fits into your schedule.
- Never stop creating. Revamp your site every so often. Post something new as often as you can.
- Never "explain" or make apologies for the work in your portfolio — let the images speak for themselves. If something more needs saying, let your interviewer ask and then respond as needed. If they express appreciation for an image, just smile and say "Thank you," and add nothing more.
- Always keep your demo reels and portfolio site up to date.
- Whatever you have to do to feel most creative and inspired — go do it! Do what you love, and do it often.

Thanks to Randy Briley, Caleb Parrish, Mathias Takacs, Dominic Sodano, Katie Orcutt, and Mark Ferrari for sharing their tips and insights.

CHAPTER NINE
Interviewing for jobs

I was late, and I was lost. The job interview was scheduled for 3:00 p.m., but it was already 3:15 and I couldn't find the studio's office for the life of me — instead, I found myself driving around the block in circles, wondering why none of the building addresses matched up with the address I was looking for. When I finally realized my mistake, I parked my car and raced into the interview room, now 32 minutes late. There was a panel of five interviewers waiting for me. At first, they were visibly annoyed at my tardiness. But then they broke into laughter, as I turned red, looked down, and realized I wasn't wearing any pants!

Then, fortunately, I woke up. It was just a bad dream — a "stress dream" that I've had several times over the years. The fact that my subconscious mind repeatedly plays that ridiculous scenario when I sleep is a testament to just how stressful the interview process can be. Although, in real life, the anticipation of an upcoming interview is usually much worse than the actual interview itself.

This chapter will help you understand the various types of interviews, and how to best prepare yourself for the challenge. As nightmarish as it may seem, you need to ace your interviews if you want to land your dream job.

How should I prepare for a phone interview?

When a game company likes your résumé, the next step is to schedule a phone interview. It's a quick and low-risk way for the hiring manager to decide whether to bring you in for a longer on-site interview, so the stakes are high — it's your first and best chance to make a strong personal impression.

I can not overstate the importance of this call! Phone interviews are usually quite short, usually under a half hour, so you don't have much time to make your case. For the best chance of progressing to the next stage of the interview process, there are three important things you should do to prepare.

The first is to research the company. In a typical job search, you'll apply to several different companies, and you might be more excited about some than others. But companies don't want employees who are simply passionate about making games — they want people who are passionate about *their company*, specifically. If an interviewer senses that you don't care about the company, they'll pass you by for someone who does. So research the company before the phone call to learn as much as you can: the games they've made, recent news or publicity, even the names and careers of their top game designers and other employees. The interviewer may ask questions to test your knowledge and interest, such as "Why are you interested in working for this company?" Or, "Why are you excited about our games?" Be sure to think of good answers to those questions before the call, or you're unlikely to get the job.

The second thing is to come up with what I call your "unique sales pitch" for why you'd be a good fit for the company. Use it to help the interviewer understand how your specific skills and talents will help you succeed in the job. If it looks like you're getting towards the end of the call and you haven't yet been able to talk about your unique sales pitch, tell the interviewer that you want to be sure you get to explain your thoughts about the position, and ask if it would be okay to discuss it now.

It might take some focused thought to come up with your pitch. If you're having trouble, ask a friend or a family member to help — they might see some talents in you that you haven't noticed yourself, and could help you focus those into your pitch. An example might be: "I'm a self-motivated game artist, proven by the two indie games that I've worked on in my spare time." Or it could be something like "I'm a detail-oriented and trustworthy person, which is important to my future success as a tester. I have proven this at my previous job, where my manager trusted me to perform the duties each night to close down the store and deposit the day's cash in the bank."

Lastly, make sure you take the call from somewhere quiet, free of distractions, and with a reliable phone connection. I recommend taking the call from a landline instead of a cell phone if you can. As a hiring manager myself, I can't tell you how many phone interviews I've done where the candidate's voice cut out repeatedly, or the call got dropped and I had to call back. It's distracting, and can indicate that you're not good at preparing. Worst of all, it wastes valuable time on a short interview.

Also, take the call from someplace where parents, pets, and roommates won't be distractions. It's best to call from a room with a closed door, and you can even hang a little sign to let everybody know not to disturb you. Then you'll be able to focus all of your attention on the call, avoid wasting valuable time, and make a strong and lasting first impression.

I can't get hired at a new job, what am I doing wrong?

I received this question from an experienced game developer who lost his job when the company went out of business. He'd been hunting for a new job for over a year, with no luck. I could certainly empathize with him — anybody who's done an extended job hunt knows it's frustrating and demoralizing, not to mention hard on your finances.

No matter who you are, every successful job hunt follows the same process: find a job to target, send an application, do some interviews, and get a job offer. If the process isn't going well for you, the key is to figure out which step is falling apart and then fix it.

Finding a job opening is the easiest step, because game companies post their jobs online. Start with a job board aggregator like Indeed.com or Monster.com, or go directly to the game company website. If you can't find any job openings near where you live, you may need to broaden your search to other cities, states, or even countries if you live somewhere that doesn't have many game studios.

Applying for a job is the next step. If you're applying but not getting replies, or if you're getting rejection letters, then you have one of two problems: either you're applying for jobs that don't fit you, or you need to improve your résumé. Double-check to make sure you're applying for jobs that are a close match for your skills and experience. A good rule of thumb is to only apply to jobs when you match at least 80% of the requirements listed in the job description. Make sure that your résumé adequately explains your experience, and that it does a good job of selling the company on what you can offer them as an employee. Do a thoughtful overhaul of your résumé with those things in mind.

The next step is interviewing, which many people struggle with. Are you getting interviews, but then they're not calling you back? Or they're calling, but only to say that you're not the right fit? In that case, a few things could be going wrong.

First, you might need to polish up your interviewing skills. There are a number of articles and YouTube videos to guide you in becoming a better interviewee, so if you've never done any research on how to do a good interview, get on it! Some of the main questions to honestly ask yourself include: Am I doing a good job of communicating my skills and experience to the interviewers? Am I exuding a positive attitude, and a positive outlook on my life and my work? Am I leaving my interviewers with a sense that I'm a dependable and friendly person they'd want to have on their team?

There's another reason you might be getting interviews but not job offers, and this one doesn't have anything to do with your interviewing skills, but with your résumé. If your résumé is blustery or contains "little white lies" about your skills, or otherwise paints you to be more talented or experienced than you really are at this point in your career, then you might be getting interviews for jobs you aren't actually qualified for. Sure, put your best foot forward on your résumé. But if you overstate yourself too much, you'll be found out in the interview and you won't get the job — you'll only get embarrassed.

There's one last reason you might not be getting hired: you simply might not be a good fit for the companies you applied to. It can take a while to find the right fit — timing is everything, and sometimes it's a matter of luck. Hang in there.

What is an "informal" interview?

Informal interviews are like ninjas: they can sneak up on you when you least expect it, and by the time you know what's going on, it's already too late.

For example, let's say you're attending a game conference like PAX or GDC, and you're at an after-party, talking to somebody you've just met over drinks. They start asking perfectly normal questions like "what do you do?" or "what kind of job do you want after you graduate?"

Maybe they're just making friendly small talk... but maybe not. They could be a recruiter, a hiring manager, or somebody influential from a game studio who's been asked to scope out promising candidates. What if they're asking questions to assess whether they want to work with you?

In other words, you're being informally interviewed!

The first step is to realize that you're actually in an interview situation. Stay cool. Keep your responses short and focused. Don't ramble — it's better to give a shorter response and then let them ask for more if they want to dig deeper.

Informal interviews can happen when you least expect it, so the best way to be prepared is to prepare ahead of time. Think about how you'll answer when they ask about your career aspirations, talents, and skills. Write it down and practice it like a little sales pitch. You don't want your responses to sound scripted, but you're likely to ramble if you haven't prepared and practiced.

If you tend to get nervous or flustered when talking about yourself, practice on your family or friends. Or, practice in front of a mirror (it sounds weird, but it actually works). While you're practicing your pitch, also practice standing up straight, talking clearly, and looking the other person in the eye. As they say, "practice makes perfect."

Lastly, it doesn't do much good to have an informal interview if you don't build an honest connection with the interviewer. Always carry a clean, wrinkle-free business card to hand them at the end of the conversation. And if they ask you to send them your portfolio or résumé, remember to do it! Don't wait — send it the very next day.

What should I expect during an on-site interview?

At last, the on-site interview. If you've been through multiple rounds of informal interviews and phone calls, this is the "big interview" you've been working toward. The on-site takes place at the game studio, and can last anywhere from a few hours to an entire day.

This formal interview often starts with a tour of the studio and team areas, to "warm you up" and become more comfortable in the interview — but it's also a chance for them to sell you on their company ("Isn't this place cool? Wouldn't you love to work here?"). Pay attention, ask questions if anything interesting catches your eye, and try to imagine what it might feel like to work in this studio with these people.

When the interview portion starts in earnest, you'll be seated in a conference room with a single person or a group of interviewers. This is when things get serious, and they'll ask you the "hard questions" that you'll need to prepare for ahead of time. They may ask technical questions like "Explain how a hash table works" (don't worry, artists, that question is for programmers only), or behavioral questions like "Tell us about a time when you had to work effectively with a difficult co-worker." If they ask questions that you can't answer, do your best to talk through it, and be upfront about what you know and what you don't. It's okay to get a few questions wrong, and some don't even have correct answers — they're just trying to understand how you think about the problem.

Toward the end of the interview, you might be asked whether you have any questions for them. This is a great opportunity for you to ask about the studio culture, what it's like to work there, or why they personally like the studio. Consider preparing a few questions ahead of time based on your research, because then you'll learn some helpful information while also demonstrating your knowledge of the company and their games.

One last thing: It's critical to remember that they're not just assessing your job skills, but also your personality and "team fit." Most of the interviewers are programmers, producers, artists, and other gamers just like you — so present yourself like somebody they'd want to work with. Be sure to dress the part and nail the interview questions, but also convey a positive attitude. Be friendly. Remember to smile.

Why do some interviewers look for "team fit"?

Companies want to hire people who are talented, but they also want employees who get along with their teams — employees who contribute to a positive company culture at all times, whether that's while working, crunching, watching movies, playing games, or debating the game design in a heated team meeting. They know they'll be spending long and stressful hours with you someday. So if you want them to hire you, convince them you're fun to work with and that you'd make a great team member day in and day out.

But don't stress about it. The best approach is to just be yourself and let your true personality show through during the interview. Show them that you're smart, funny, friendly, generous, and passionate. If you're somebody that *you'd* want to work with, chances are good they'll want to work with you too.

What should I wear to an interview?

Game studios are a lot like other tech companies: Casual. But when you add video game culture into the mix, things can get weird.

I used to work with an amazing programmer who wore the same ripped-up shorts and ancient T-shirts every day, and with an amazing artist who sometimes came to work wearing a miniskirt and cat ears. So, let's just say, the game industry is a little bit different. How should you dress, knowing that your interviewers could be wearing shorts and flip-flops, or sporting a tanuki tail?

There are a few basics that apply to any job interview. Make sure your clothing isn't worn out or wrinkled. Pay attention to your personal hygiene — get a haircut, trim your fingernails, take a shower, wash your hair. Shave. Go easy on the perfume or cologne.

Dark slacks, dresses, skirts, or decent-looking jeans are fine (no rips or holes), but don't wear shorts. A button-down shirt or sweater is a safe bet, or if you have a gamer-geek shirt or other clothing, it can be a great way to express yourself and connect with your interviewers (just make sure it's in good condition and in good taste). Wear shoes that are clean, casual and closed-toe.

Those are guidelines, but every company is different. An easy way to find out how to dress for any specific company is to ask them. Call or email your contact at the company and ask how you should dress for the interview, and they'll give you suggestions based on their company's specific culture and expectations.

First impressions count. Your interviewers' first impressions of you might start the minute you walk through the door, so don't miss your opportunity to dress for success.

Do I need to follow up after the interview?

When you've finished going through the informal, phone interview, and formal interviews, it's a good idea to send a thank-you note. Just a simple message, something like "Thank you for the opportunity to interview with [company name] yesterday. I enjoyed meeting the team and learning more about the studio, and I'm hopeful we can start building amazing games together sometime soon."

You can send it by email, but mailing a hand-written thank-you card (an actual card, made of actual paper) will stand out and leave a good impression. Whatever you do, don't wait — send it the very next day.

I got rejected, what should I do next?

So you've been sending out your résumé, doing phone interviews, maybe an on-site interview with a company you're excited about. Things seem to be going great, until you get that dreaded email: "Thank you for your interest in our company. Unfortunately, you're not good enough. Not smart enough. Not talented enough. Goodbye, and don't come back."

Okay, that was a dramatization. Real rejection letters are more tactful, usually something like "Thanks for your interest but we've decided to pursue other candidates." But it can still feel terrible. You've been rejected! You're bummed out, frustrated, maybe starting to feel a bit hopeless.

Take a deep breath, and ask yourself how you can learn from the experience. Even when you've been turned down, you can spin it into a learning opportunity: What did you learn about the company? About the industry? What new networking connections did you make? What have you discovered about your skills, compared to what the hiring manager was expecting? Interviewing is a skill in itself, so don't think of it as rejection — think of it as practice. You'll do better next time.

Keep in mind that rejection is a normal part of every job search. Each company is looking for a different mix of skill, talent and personality, so it's a statistical fact that you won't be a perfect match for most of the jobs you apply for. Job hunts typically take three to six months before a job offer, so it requires endurance, perseverance, and a focus on succeeding in the long run. Work on your hunt methodically and relentlessly, and you'll have the best chance of snagging an opportunity right when it becomes available.

I promise you, there's an awesome job out there that's a perfect fit for your skills, talents, and personality. So quit moping around. Get back on the hunt and track it down.

CHAPTER TEN
Career networking

When I got my first job at a game studio, it was largely thanks to my friend Michelle. I didn't have any experience testing games, but she knew I was a hard worker and a passionate gamer, so she talked with her manager and recommended he call me in for an interview. He did just that — and then he hired me. The rest is history. That job became my first stepping stone in a long career at the studio, culminating in a position as the company's studio head twelve years later.

After that, my next job at an e-commerce company was made possible largely because I was friends with the CEO. He'd been trying to hire me ever since he started the company, so when I was laid off from my job at the game studio, he was ready with an offer to come and work for him as a senior product manager.

And when I was ready to get back into the game industry a few years later, I sent a text message to an old co-worker who was running a new, unannounced project team. He happened to have a job opening that he thought would be a perfect fit, so I applied for the job and was contacted for an interview within a week.

When you read those anecdotes about how I got each of my jobs, do you see a pattern? In case it's not obvious, I'll call it out for you: In each example, I already knew a person inside the company, and that person played a key role in helping me land the job.

Don't get me wrong — healthy companies don't just give jobs to their friends without taking them through a rigorous process of applying and interviewing. I still had to jump through the typical hoops, and I definitely wouldn't have been hired if I wasn't a good fit for the job. But having those recommendations from the inside helped me stand out from the crowd of dozens (maybe hundreds!) of others who may have been competing for the same jobs.

In other words, having the right skills is only part of the equation. If you really want to stand out, you also need to know people inside the company. But how do you get to know people inside a company in the first place?

The answer is, career networking. If you learn to do it, and if you do it consistently, and if you do it well, there's no end to the opportunities that open up throughout your career. But if you don't, I promise that you're in for a long, difficult job hunt. So read on, and pay attention, because this could be the difference between landing your dream job, or settling for much less.

What is career networking?

Career networking, also called professional networking, is simply the process of making personal connections with people in your industry, with the hope that you may have the opportunity to help each other out someday. It's usually done through short meetings over coffee or drinks, or at industry events like conferences or meet-ups.

When you're looking for a new job, your overall goal for career networking is to gather information that will help you get a job. But the mechanics are simple: you meet people, chat about things you're both interested in, and learn about the game industry along the way. If their company has any job openings that might be good for you, and if they think you'd be a good person to work with, then they're likely to help you get the job.

If you're new to the career world, networking with people you don't know might seem scary, manipulative, or even impossible — if you're an introvert, you might be cringing at the very thought! But it's actually a simple process that's good for everyone involved, and can have a huge payoff for your career. It can even be fun.

Plus, it's a virtuous cycle. Someday, when you're well-connected yourself, you can pay it forward by networking with newbies and helping them find their very first jobs in the industry the same way you did.

Is it hard to get a job if I don't have a big network?

If you don't have a big network, or if you don't know many people in the game industry just yet, don't worry — you'll still be able to get a job. But it will be harder and it will take longer, so it's well worth the time and effort to start building your professional network now.

One of the major benefits of career networking is that it engages your allies to help you with your search. People enjoy helping each other out. When you meet new people and they get to know you, they'll enjoy sharing tips and suggesting jobs or companies that you should look into. And if you're lucky, you might even meet the very person who can hire you.

Another reason to build a network of people that you know inside of game studios is that it helps you get access to the many "hidden" jobs. At any given time, there are dozens of job openings that game studios haven't yet published to the public, for various reasons. Does that surprise you? It's absolutely true. Those hidden jobs are there, and you can find out about them and apply before anyone else does, if you have a strong professional network helping you out.

How can I start networking if I'm new to the industry?

The best way to grow your professional network is to start with your current network: the people you already know. Make a list of everyone you know who is somehow related to the game industry, including teachers, developers, recruiters, and classmates who recently got jobs. Anybody who can offer advice or introduce you to others in the game industry should go on your list.

Then, start calling and messaging those contacts and ask to meet them for lunch or coffee. (Here in Seattle, people meet for coffee any time of the day.) You should be up-front about why you want to meet, and what your goals are: you want to learn more about the game industry, and you want introductions to new people who could help you get a job. Here's an example email to get you started:

"Hi Meghan. What have you been up to? I'm graduating this year so I'm gathering info about game studios I might want to work at. Since you're in the game industry, I'm hoping you might have some info or advice for me.

(I'm not asking for a job or anything, I'm just trying to learn more about the industry and make some new contacts.) Would you have time to meet me for lunch or coffee next week?"

When you get a meeting, use your time wisely because it can go quickly. Keep these goals in mind:

- Thank the person for meeting with you
- Give them a one-minute summary of your skills, talents, and the types of jobs you're interested in
- Ask for their opinion on which game studios they think you should be targeting in your job search
- Ask them to suggest the names of two or three other people (especially at those studios) who they wouldn't mind introducing you to via email

Any tips or advice they offer could be helpful, so listen carefully and don't be afraid to write it all down (your friend will probably be flattered). It's also important to get some additional names so you can continue to grow your network. For each name you get during your meetings, add them to your original list, then reach out and ask for their help as a referral from your previous contact:

"Hi Mr. Gordons, our mutual friend Meghan Smith thought you'd be a good person to talk to about finding a job as a [programmer/artist/whatever]. I'm graduating this year so I'm trying to learn more about the industry, and about whether your company might have any applicable job openings. I'd appreciate any help or advice you can offer. Would you have time for coffee or a brief phone call next week?"

Don't forget to send follow-up emails to thank each and every person who helps you out. And, someday, when you've been in the game industry for a few years yourself, remember to keep the karma flowing by helping out a recent graduate who's working to grow their own fledgling network.

What's the best way to connect with someone on LinkedIn?

When you're searching for a job in the game industry, LinkedIn is a powerful tool for growing your network. But there are some "unwritten rules" of LinkedIn etiquette, and you can embarrass yourself if you aren't thoughtful when you invite people to Connect.

First of all, most professionals don't accept connection requests from people they don't know. LinkedIn has a fair number of spammers, which is why many users are wary about accepting connection requests from people they've never heard of. If you invite somebody who doesn't know who you are, they probably won't accept and, worse, you'll make a bad first impression. The good news is that you don't have to meet them face-to-face before they'll accept. It's perfectly okay to connect with somebody if you've met them over the phone, via email, or on a discussion forum if you've actually had a conversation with them. Just be sure they know you well enough that they won't think "who the hell are you" when they get your request.

Another gotcha is that, when you send an invitation to connect, it defaults to a generic message that could make your request seem like spam. So instead of using the default message, take a minute to write a custom message to show your new connection that you aren't just spamming people — you care about connecting on a more personal level. It also gives you a chance to remind them where you met or what you have in common. Here are some examples, feel free to rip them off and customize as needed:

"Hi, John. We met at GDC last week, and I enjoyed talking with you about Bay Area micro-brews. I'm just getting started in the game industry, and would love to stay in touch in case we can work together someday. Take care, Bailey Smith."

"Good morning! Thank you for visiting my school to tell us about your game studio. The information was really helpful for students who are just starting out. It would be great to stay in touch so I can return the favor some day! Sincerely, Mike Jones."

"Hi Sandeep, thank you for the advice you gave me yesterday about how to improve my online art portfolio. I've already taken your advice to heart and am updating my layout today. I'd love to stay in touch, maybe we can work together someday."

Notice how each example reminds your contact where you met, then makes a personal connection and explains why you want to stay in touch. It's as simple as that.

How should I use LinkedIn to stay in touch with my contacts?

The whole point of LinkedIn is to stay in touch with professionals you've met so you can add value to each others' careers and lives. But with relationships on LinkedIn, just as in the real world, you need to nurture them or they'll fade.

If you're just starting out in your career, you might feel like you don't have much to offer yet. That's okay — you've got your whole life ahead of you, so there's plenty of time to give back once you're more established. In the meantime, LinkedIn's activity feed makes it easy to stay in touch and let your connections know you're thinking about them.

There are several ways you can leverage the feed to stay in touch. When somebody posts an article or status that you like, let them know by clicking "Like" or leaving a comment. When you see that somebody gets a new job or a promotion, send them a message to say congratulations, and ask how they've been doing lately. If you find a link or article that you think people in your network would like, then share it.

And whenever you get some value from a connection — if you've learned something from them, or they've helped you out in any way — send them a quick message to thank them and let them know how much they've helped you. It will strengthen your connection, and it will make their day.

Do you have any networking tips for shy or introverted people?

There are many different ways to do networking — if you're shy or introverted, you just need to approach it in a way that's comfortable for you. If you don't like big crowds, then you don't need to squeeze yourself into over-crowded industry conventions; instead, do your networking one-on-one over lunch. If you don't like loud, bustling bars, then don't have your meetings at a club; instead, meet at your favorite quiet and cozy coffee shop.

If you're more comfortable talking with new people online, you can also do a lower-pressure version of networking by participating in online communities. I think you should still do in-person meetings, because nothing builds connection like a face-to-face conversation. But you can also meet interesting and helpful game industry people on art forums, message boards, social media groups, coder Q&A sites, and other online communities. There are also groups such as Women Who Code that support under-represented groups in tech, so try searching online to find similar communities that might interest you.

If you're short on confidence, then let me assure you that confident networking comes with practice. I've seen the most painfully shy people grow their confidence, and their network, just by taking it one meeting at a time. As you learn more about the game industry, jobs, and companies, you'll feel less like an industry outsider and more like an insider. That confidence will show through during your job interviews, and put you ahead of all the other candidates who don't have the inside scoop.

CHAPTER ELEVEN
Relocating to take a job

In the old days, young people dreamed of escaping the backwater confines of their small town and moving to Hollywood to "make it big" in music or movies. Many still do. It's a compelling story (itself the topic of songs and movies, so meta!) but for most of those small-town girls and boys, the reality is a much different story — I've personally known several who moved to Los Angeles or New York but ended up waiting tables for a few years before giving up and moving back home. For dreamers who aren't prepared for the hardship and hustle, the big city has a way of chewing them up and spitting them out.

Fortunately, the game industry is significantly more stable and predictable than the dog-eat-dog (and slowly declining) music or movie businesses. But it's similar in that most game jobs are located in the world's largest cities. In fact, there might not be any game studios at all in your current city, state, or even your entire country, depending on where you live. The thought of uprooting your life and moving to a new city to take your first game job may seem scary, but it's often the best strategy for starting your career.

Even in the big cities, employers know that there are talented developers across the country and around the world, so they routinely look to smaller towns for qualified candidates to bring in. And that's why it's common for game developers to search for jobs outside of the city where they're currently living, and then relocate to one of the many game development "hotbed" cities to take a job and start a career.

If you hadn't considered relocation before, at this point you may be asking yourself: What happens if I move to a new city, but then it takes weeks or months to find a job? How will I pay for rent and other expenses without any income? What if I can't find a job, go broke, and end up living huddled under a bridge eating instant ramen for the rest of my life?

Don't worry — none of that will happen if you develop a good job-search strategy and do things in the right order. That's the focus of this chapter.

Should I move to a bigger city to get a game job?

In general, big cities aren't necessarily "better" than smaller ones. In fact, even though jobs in cities seem to pay higher salaries compared to smaller towns, the high costs of city living may burn through your paycheck faster than you expect. Then why risk it? Because many of those big cities are game development "hotbeds" — they're home to more game studios, and therefore more game jobs, than anywhere else. It's important for you to consider moving to a hotbed, for several reasons.

First, cities with several game studios are good for your long-term career security. Even if your game studio has a layoff or goes out of business, you'll get a new job faster and easier because other game companies are nearby. People who lose their job in a game development hotbed can often find a new one in a matter of days, because even when one studio is laying people off, others are hiring.

Another reason is because game dev hotbed cities tend to attract the industry's top talent. How does that benefit you? As someone just starting your career, chances are good that you'll be working with some of the best artists, designers, and programmers in the country — maybe even the world. Working alongside top talent is one of the best possible ways to learn and advance your career, so working at a studio in a game dev hotbed can put you on the fast track to career success.

The third reason is that game dev hotbeds fuel the growth of new game studios in the area. When a group of professional game developers or investors considers opening a new game studio, one of their top considerations is the ability to easily (and quickly) hire experienced, talented people. Game dev hotbed cities have more game developers than anywhere else, so they're an obvious choice. That's why game dev hotbeds offer more job opportunities for you: there are more companies available for you to work at, now and in the future.

Which cities are game dev hotbeds? In the U.S., the top cities are San Francisco, Austin, Los Angeles, Seattle, and Chicago. Internationally, the top hotbed cities in the world are Tokyo, London, San Francisco, Austin, and Montreal. But there are smaller game dev hotbeds all around the world, so don't limit yourself. Search the Web for "game dev hotbeds" to find even more game-centric cities you could use to launch your career.

Should I move first, or find a job first?

If you decide to relocate to a new city to start your career, that's great — but you don't want to end up far away from home with no job and no income. So it's usually best to wait until you actually you receive, and accept, a formal job offer.

It's perfectly acceptable to apply for jobs in cities outside of your current town, state, or country. You can do the interviews over the phone or using video chat software like Skype, and you can travel to the other city by car, bus, or airplane to do in-person interviews. Sometimes the company interviewing you will even pay for your flights and meals, so your out-of-pocket costs for the trip would be nearly zero. Traveling for an interview can be fun, especially if you stay a couple of extra days to explore the city and discover whether you could see yourself starting a new life there someday.

How will the cost of living affect my salary?

In the United States, about half of all people live in small towns or rural areas. If you're one of them, you might be looking with envy at the relatively higher salary averages offered by bigger metropolitan areas like New York or Los Angeles. Should you consider leaving your comfort zone and moving to a big, coastal metro area for a chance at a bigger paycheck?

It's true that bigger cities usually offer higher pay than smaller towns. Sometimes it's a lot more. However, the fat paycheck comes with strings attached: those cities pay more because they have a significantly higher cost of living.

"Cost of living" is the idea that living expenses such as rent, home prices, groceries, transportation, and other basics, can all cost more in certain cities compared to others. For example, the cost of renting an apartment in San Francisco is more than double the cost of an apartment in Houston, Texas. That's why companies in San Francisco pay a higher salary than companies in Houston — San Francisco is expensive, so if they want to attract workers to live there, they need to offset the higher living costs by paying higher salaries.

What does that mean for you? It means that even though a game company in San Francisco may pay a bigger salary than a company in Texas, it might actually be worth less after you factor in the amount you'll be paying every month for San Francisco's expensive rent, food, transportation, and everything else you spend money on to live your daily life.

An excellent resource for comparing salaries and costs of living is Payscale.com, a free site that lets you type in the salary that's offered by two jobs in two cities, and view the difference in cost of living between them. You can also search the Web for "cost of living calculator" and you'll find several useful tools. Just remember, when you're comparing job salaries between cities, be sure to factor in the differences in the costs of living — otherwise, that fancy city salary might just put you in the poorhouse.

Do I need a special visa to work in the U.S.?

To work in the U.S. as a non-citizen, you'll need to obtain a special permit from the U.S. government called a work visa. Most game developers get a specialty occupation visa called an H-1B, but there are strict regulations to qualify. You need to meet at least three major requirements: you must have a bachelor's degree or higher; you must be working in a "specialty occupation" under U.S. visa policies; and you must already have a prospective employer in the U.S. to arrange to apply for the visa on your behalf. That last point is important, because it essentially requires you to receive a job offer from a U.S. company before you can get an H-1B visa.

The company's human resources department is likely to assist you with the legal and visa paperwork, or they may even do it all for you. To learn more, go to the U.S. Citizenship and Immigration Services website at www.uscis.gov, or the U.S. Embassy website for your current country.

Note that if you're relocating along with your husband, wife, or significant other, they'll need to get a work visa of their own. If they don't qualify for an H1-B, there are other types of visas that you could try to get for them, such as a student visa or other special work visa. Be sure to think about your significant other's prospects for the new country as well, and plan accordingly.

What are some tips for relocating to a foreign country?

The idea of leaving your home and moving to a new country and culture could be exciting or terrifying, depending on your personal disposition. It may not be the right move for everybody, but for the more adventurous spirits, it can open you up to new job opportunities and could be one of the most educational and rewarding experiences of your career.

If you do take the leap, work as hard as you can to learn about your new country's language and culture before you move there, and take frequent language lessons before and after you move. Even if you're moving from one English-speaking country to another, it wouldn't hurt to do a little research — even UK and U.S. English have different vocabulary, spelling, and especially different slang.

It's a good idea to arrive in the new country several days before your start date, just to relax, explore the neighborhood, and let your jet lag subside before you start your brand-new job. Keep an open mind, and be patient in social situations until you get accustomed to what is and is not considered rude — either to locals or to you. And if it takes a while before you start to feel like you fit in, don't let it bother you — be patient while you learn your new language and culture. All the effort will be worth it.

If I land a job in a new city, can I get help with moving costs?

It's common for game developers to move to a new city to take a new job, but moving across the country (or the world!) can be expensive. You'll need to buy packing supplies; you may need to ship furniture and boxes; you may need a moving van, or airplane tickets, or gas for your car. If you live in a house, you may need to pay professional movers to transport your furniture. If you're moving far from where you live, you may need to pay for hotels and meals during a multi-day trip. It can add up quickly, and if you're fresh out of school, you might not have enough money saved up to pay for it all.

Luckily, your new employer may help out with some, or all, of those expenses. First of all, they might have a relocation benefit as part of their standard benefits package — but they don't always mention it unless you ask. If they didn't mention it as part of the job offer, call or email the recruiter or the human resources person who helped you schedule your interviews, and ask them about it: "Does the company offer relocation assistance for new employees?" It could be as easy as that to get what's essentially free money to help you pay your moving costs.

If the company doesn't have a relocation benefit, another tactic is to ask for a moving stipend to be included as part of your job offer. When you receive your initial job offer, you can counter offer and ask them to add some help with your moving expenses. Most employers will agree to add up to a thousand dollars to your job offer, depending on how far you're moving to take the job. Note that most companies will add conditions on that money; for example, they might require you to repay it if you quit the job within a year. But normally you'd expect to stay longer than a year anyway, so it's a reasonable tradeoff.

It costs game companies a lot to find talented developers. By the time they found you and made an offer, they've already spent dozens of hours searching, sourcing and interviewing people. You might not have confidence in your abilities if you're new to the industry, but I promise you that if a company has made you a job offer, they have confidence in you and are quite willing to make an investment. So don't be shy about asking for relocation expenses, because the worst that can happen is that they say no. In most parts of the world, helping employees with moving expenses is a normal part of doing business. They'll usually say yes.

CHAPTER TWELVE
Alternative work situations

The nature of work has changed dramatically over the years. If you had been alive back in 1870, there's a good chance you'd be working in the agriculture industry, because nearly half of all Americans were employed by agriculture. But over the course of the following century, the employment landscape began to shift. Agricultural work was largely replaced by manufacturing work, which is now being replaced by "white-collar" office work.

If you're under the age of forty-ish, you probably take the Internet for granted. But from a historical perspective, the Internet is quite new — and it's enabling the highly-connected, always-on, speed-of-thought communication that's fueling a new shift in the employment landscape from "office work" to "anywhere work."

Most of game development still happens in an office. But there are other work situations that have started to take hold, such as freelancing, independent game development, gig employment, and perhaps others that are just beginning to form. They may not work for everyone, but these alternative work situations are worth knowing about in case they might work for you.

What's the difference between full-time and freelancing?

The difference between employees, contractors, and freelancers can be confusing. Even people inside the industry get confused and use the wrong terminology, so let's clarify here:

- An employee is a person who works for a single company exclusively, with no set date at which the employment will end. Employees usually receive a fixed salary or hourly wage, and other financial benefits such as health insurance. This is by far the most common way for people to work in the game industry.
- A freelancer is a person who has a legal contract promising to work for a company for a fixed amount of time and an agreed-upon amount of money. Freelancers are allowed to work for multiple companies at a time, which is why they're also called "independent contractors."

How does the choice affect you? First, companies do not pay for health benefits for freelancers, so you'll need to sign up for health insurance and pay out of your own pocket. Health insurance could cost hundreds of dollars each month, and you'll want to pay it even when you're between jobs and might not have any income.

Freelancers also need to pay their own taxes. When you're an employee, the company automatically takes the appropriate taxes out of your paycheck, and they might even foot the bill for certain taxes on your behalf. But as a freelancer, you must remember to pay taxes on your own, and you may also be responsible for "self-employment" taxes. So if you go the freelance route, be sure to understand the nuances of your state and federal tax obligations so you don't get into legal trouble.

The last key difference between employees and freelancers is in job stability. As an employee, you don't need to worry about where your next game project is coming from — it's the company's job to start new projects and keep you busy. But as a freelancer, you always need to be searching for your next job, even while you're working on your current one. You'll spend part of each week wearing your "salesman" hat: networking, advertising, sending out your portfolio, answering requests for work bids. If you don't line up your next gig before you finish your current one, you'll have an unpaid gap between projects. Some freelancers improve their financial stability by working on multiple projects at the same time, which can be harrowing.

Note that employment law can differ from region to region. I'm not a lawyer, so consider talking to an attorney or other legal expert before making any decision that would affect your employment and your income.

Should I consider becoming a freelancer?

When you work as a freelancer, you're a one-person business. You're responsible for paying your own taxes and health insurance, and for drumming up new business in the form of contracts to work on game projects. If that doesn't sound like something you'd excel at, or if job instability scares you or stresses you out, then freelancing might not be for you.

Why would anybody want to become a freelancer? First of all, the money is good — freelancers usually get paid more per hour than full-time game company employees. For example, I know some freelance game programmers who charge over $100 per hour, which is much more than they'd make as regular full-time employees.

Then there's the flexibility of working when you want, where you want, how you want, and on projects that you choose. You're your own boss, and many people prefer that lifestyle. They feel that the freedom and independence of being an independent contractor more than outweighs the other annoyances and uncertainty.

Finally, some jobs in the game industry can be hard to get as a full-time employee. Jobs like music composer, sound engineer, and writing jobs are traditionally handled by freelancers. So if you're looking to do one of those jobs, you might consider freelancing at some point in your career because full-time employment in those jobs is hard to find.

I say "at some point in your career" because, if you're new to the game industry, I do not recommend starting out as a freelancer. You'll find it difficult to get hired for freelance jobs unless you've already shipped a few games, because game companies won't risk hiring a freelancer without a track record. If you start by working full-time in a game studio for a few years, you'll build a professional network that will play a key role in helping you find work when you become a freelancer later on. As a full-timer on a game team, you'll gain experience, grow your skills mastery, and build an impressive portfolio of shipped titles.

There's another reason to start with full-time work: it will give you a chance to save up a financial safety net in case you ever become unemployed between freelance gigs. As a new freelancer, it could take months of effort before you're booked solid, so a little extra padding in your bank account could be a necessity.

The most successful freelancers I know started as employees, got some experience, built their professional network, and then tried their hand at freelancing after building financial stability. Some of them weren't up for the freelance lifestyle and quickly went back to work full-time, but some are still successful freelancers, years later. Either way, it was a learning experience and an adventure.

I'm still a temp, why won't my team hire me full-time?

Many game studios like to hire new people as temporary ("temp") workers, to make sure they can do a good job before extending a permanent job offer. Think of it as a "try before you buy" plan for the company. But getting hired full-time isn't guaranteed, and some companies choose to repeatedly extend the temp contract rather than making a commitment. If you're getting hired for temp work but still haven't been offered a permanent job, what can you do?

The best approach is to have a candid talk with people you work with on the team, especially your manager. Try to get insight into why the company isn't making the commitment. Maybe it's because the team expects the job to be temporary, and they won't need anybody to do the work after a certain date — companies also use temp workers when they only need the employee for a short time. But maybe there's something you can learn about your work style or your communication style, or some other aspect of your work that makes the team feel that you aren't a good long-term fit, hopefully something you could improve over time.

So reach out to your manager or others on the team whom you trust and have a good relationship with. Whether you schedule lunch or coffee with them or you do it over email, be open to their input. Listen for any tips that you could use to improve the way you work. And then take that advice to heart and put it into your daily practice, so that you'll have a better chance of getting hired full-time, next time around.

Should I work as an indie developer, or work for a company?

When I was a kid, everybody dreamed of starting their own rock band, but young people these days seem to be more interested in starting their own independent ("indie") game companies. Maybe those two goals don't seem related, but they're alike for at least one reason: you wouldn't quit your job or drop out of school to start a new band, and I don't recommend dropping everything to start your own indie game studio, either.

Bands and game studios are both crushingly difficult endeavors that require a huge amount of talent, experience, and business skill to do successfully. Just as you wouldn't expect to create a successful band before you learned to play the guitar, you won't be able to create a successful game studio before you learn how to make games.

But if you've already learned how to make games, for example by working at an established game company for a few years to learn the trade, then you'll have a much better chance at succeeding as an indie. That's exactly what some of my friends did when they started Crazy Viking Studios — they worked in the industry for a decade before striking out on their own. Even then, it was a much harder challenge than they ever imagined, and it took them eighteen months, often working six to seven days a week, to ship their first successful game.

That's why I recommend doing indie development purely as a hobby on evenings and weekends, until you put in some time to level up your professional game development skills. Once you reach a master level, then you can decide whether you're up for the challenge of hiring a team, designing a game, building it, marketing it, and supporting it — all while trying to run a successful business. Indie development is not for the faint of heart.

CHAPTER THIRTEEN
Succeeding at your job

Searching for a new job can be a full-time job in itself — writing your résumé, building your portfolio, networking with people in the industry, interviewing, interviewing, then interviewing some more. It's a lot of effort, but it's nothing compared to what comes next. How much thought have you given to how you'll succeed once you finally land the job?

If you're in the mood to take a short break from the job hunt, let's fast-forward to a time, not far from now, when your search has successfully concluded and you've started your new job working at a game company. Now that you're in, the next challenge is to do your job well and grow your career for years to come. Let's talk about how to succeed, now and in the future.

Is it better to be a specialist or a generalist?

If you look at my personal career, you might guess that I'm a generalist. I've done a lot of different jobs: artist, tester, designer, programmer, technical director, studio head, product manager — I've clearly embraced a generalist lifestyle.

Generalists can play many roles on a team, because they're good at learning new skills. But they can also be distractible, chasing the hottest new techniques and paradigms like that dog chases squirrels in Pixar's movie *Up*. Plus, it can be hard to convince a studio to hire you just because you're "kinda good at lots of stuff."

On the other end of the scale, we have specialists. Specialists take a more focused approach — they reach a high level of achievement in a specific skill area, and eventually become experts. They often get paid more and enjoy a high degree of job security. However, that laser-focus can also be the specialist's Achilles' heel — if the studio you want to work at doesn't need people with your specialty, you might be out of luck.

That's why the best approach is to be neither a specialist nor a generalist (or, to look at it another way, to be both) by developing a "T-shaped" skill set that's both broad and deep. By depth, I mean learning a targeted skill in a specific, core discipline that you can become extremely good at. Something you're passionate about, because you'll spend thousands of hours training and honing your skill until you're an expert. Breadth is a holistic understanding of game development, an understanding of the process from start to finish and how everybody's jobs fit together. Breadth gives you insight and flexibility to support your team in different ways, and helps you communicate effectively with people in other departments and skill areas.

T-shaped is a simple concept: Start with a depth foundation, and build a breadth of understanding around it. But that's easier said than done — it takes a lot of time and effort. You may be tempted to try a bit of everything instead of developing one skill deeply, but you need to focus on a specialty and become better than anybody else who might apply to the same jobs you are. At the same time, learn about related functional areas and start developing crossover skills. If you're an animator, learn about programming — it will help you communicate with coders and write scripts to automate your grunt work. If you're a programmer, learn about game production, read a book on running a team, learn how to schedule a game team — you'll work better with your producer and it might help you land a job as a lead programmer someday.

Building a T-shaped skill set is hard work, but it will pay off by making you more valuable, adaptable, and hire-able.

What is crunch time?

Making a fresh pot of coffee at 10:00 p.m. to help me power through the remainder of the work "day." Taking a ping-pong break at midnight to get my blood flowing again. Blaring a *Rammstein* album in the office at 2:00 a.m. to amp up my programming team just enough to finish the day's features before driving home, bleary-eyed and hallucinating, and collapsing exhausted into bed.

Those are actual memories from a time in my life when I was banging out so much game code and working such long hours that I regularly returned home well after my wife had gone to sleep for the night. She used to wake just enough to say "Hi, Honey," and squint at my face in the dark. I suspect she was trying to make sure she still recognized her husband.

In the game industry, "crunch time" is real. Sometimes it's manageable — heck, sometimes it's fun, in small doses. But other times it can have a tangible, negative impact on a person's health and personal life, which is why maintaining a healthy work-life balance is a key skill for a long career in game development.

Don't get me wrong — working at a game studio is a comfortable job, even compared to other office jobs. Game developers are generally a fun, pop-culture-loving group of people, and they bring that sense of fun into the office, which you can see from the action figures, LEGOs, Nerf guns, remote controlled drones, and other "toys for grown-ups" in any game studio you walk into. It's how the relatively well-paid game developers express their interests, and how they blow off steam during the otherwise stressful periods of crunch time.

But the not-so-secret drawback of working at a game studio is that there can also be a lot of crunch time. When a game project is nearing an important deadline but is running behind schedule, the developers are expected to work overtime to get everything finished. It can mean working late nights and even working all weekend long — whatever it takes to get the job done. It's not fun, but it's common at most software companies, and even more so at game companies.

If the crunch time is short, maybe just for a week or two, it's not bad. Work-life balance for a game developer is generally comfortable, so a little bit of overtime is easy to swallow in short bursts. But when it goes on for too long, for weeks or even months, that's when it starts to cause problems with the developer's health and personal life. There are ways to help avoid crunch time, and ways to minimize it and stay healthy when it sometimes happens. But the best approach is to avoid working for "crunchy" game companies in the first place.

Why do game developers work so much overtime?

To understand overtime, start by understanding how a game team schedules their work. For any large software project, it's a best practice to break up the development timeline into smaller, manageable time periods called milestones. For each milestone, the team defines a subset of the game's features that they promise to deliver by the end of the milestone, called the milestone date.

Most milestone dates are set purely for the benefit of the game team, to help them understand whether they're staying on track throughout the months or years of development. But often times, some of the project's milestone dates are made to align with important events that exist outside of the game team's direct control.

For example, if there's a big game industry convention coming up, such as E3 (the Electronic Entertainment Expo) or GDC (the Game Developers Conference), the game team may set the conference day as a milestone date, and promise to create a working demo of the game to show off at the conference. That's important because a game's success depends largely on the free press they'll get by showing it off to journalists at conventions. But if the game team misses their milestone date and doesn't deliver the demo on time, they'll miss out on free press and their game sales might suffer.

Another example is when the game is scheduled to release on the same day as a related movie (think Harry Potter or The Hunger Games). The team can't just finish the game whenever they want to — if the game isn't ready when the movie comes out, then the game company will lose out on all the advertising and excitement of the big movie launch. It could potentially cost them millions of dollars in lost sales.

Missing an important delivery date can make or break a game, and make or break a game company. So whenever a team gets behind schedule, you can understand why developers start working extra hours to attempt to finish the project on time. Unfortunately, working too many hours can lead to sloppy work and burnout, which starts a vicious cycle: when a team misses one milestone date, it puts the future milestone dates in danger as well. If the project managers don't find a way to get the team back on track, crunch leads to more crunch, until the project is eventually completed or canceled.

As games get bigger, is crunch time getting worse?

When a game team starts to fall behind schedule, they run the risk of missing their release date. Missing a release date disappoints fans, but it can also cost the company in terms of money, goodwill, and stock price. That's why, when a game team misses an internal milestone date, it's critical to get back on track before a domino effect of missed deadlines ends in a missed release date.

One way to get a team back on track is to put them into "crunch," which is industry-speak for "working lots of overtime." The math is simple: if the team has more work than they can get done in a forty-hour week, then they may have to work more than forty hours. Developers may need to arrive at the office early and leave late, or they may need to work part- or full-time on weekends.

Crunch can last for a few days or a few weeks, depending on how far the team has fallen behind schedule. I know of a few big triple-A game projects where people on the teams were working sixty to eighty hours every week, for months at a time.

Fortunately, there are other ways a game team can get back on schedule besides crunching. One way is to reduce the scope of the game. "Scope" is an industry term referring to the size and scale of the game — the team could negotiate with management to push some scheduled features into the next milestone, or they could cut some features out of the game entirely. Or they may cleverly redesign parts of the game in a way that's equally fun to play, but doesn't take as much time and effort to create.

Another tactic is to simply change the milestone date to give the team more time to get the work done. That may only be possible if the studio's managers or the game's publisher agree to allow an extension of the game's release date, which could result in a loss of trust in the game team if the release date had already been publicly announced. So it's often only used as a last resort.

But things are getting better all the time. Every year I see game studios having less crunch time, and I think things are generally getting better. I think one reason is because the people managing game teams are becoming better at estimating and scheduling. Plus, there are better scheduling tools available, and as people in the industry get more experience estimating work and doing things like negotiating contracts and planning the work, they're getting it right more often.

How can I avoid working at a company that has a lot of overtime?

The game industry is notorious for requiring employees to work long stretches of excessive overtime, called "crunch time," which leads to a poor work-life balance for developers. But not every game company has crunch time. While poorly-run studios or teams might have crunch problems, others have strong project managers and experienced teams that know how to ship high-quality games without periods of excessive overtime.

So how can you be sure to work at a company with good project management, and avoid companies with chronic crunch? Start by researching each game company that you're interested in working for, before you accept a job offer. A good website for research is Glassdoor.com, where employees can make anonymous complaints (or, less often, compliments) about their company. If you search Glassdoor.com for a game company you're interested, you're likely to see reviews from current and past employees that could give you a sense of how well the company is managed.

You can also ask people who have worked at the company. Search Linkedin.com for people who work there currently or have in the past, and then email them (using LinkedIn) to ask their opinion. Here's an example of what to say: "Hi, I'm just starting out in the game industry, and I'm interested in possibly working at [company name]. What are your opinions about it?" If you're lucky, the employee will help you out and give you a bit of insight into the company culture. Note that you're likely to get more honesty if you ask about past companies, since employees might not feel comfortable criticizing their current workplace.

If you get an on-site interview with the company, that's actually a good time to investigate. Ask your interviewers, "How often do you guys crunch? What's your approach to a work-life balance?" When you hear their responses, listen closely and see if you can get a sense of whether crunching is a problem, or whether they have reasonable work hours. If you tour the studio before the interview, keep an eye out for signs of excessive overtime such as people looking tired and disheveled as if they've been working all night, or desks piled high with pizza boxes and empty cans of energy drink. If you see warning signs, you may want to apply to a few other companies and look for healthier options.

What are typical work hours for game teams?

Since most game employees are salaried workers, there's no punching in and out and no formal tracking of hours. There's a lot of flexibility as to which hours you work — it's up to each employee to decide when to start and stop, based on their personal needs and the needs of their game team.

Game studios generally start the work day later than most offices. Sure, some people start work as early as 7:00 a.m., but most trickle in between 9:00 and 10:00 in the morning. It's typical to take a lunch break around noon. If the studio is near any restaurants, some people might go out to eat lunch alone or with co-workers, while others might use the studio's dining area to eat a lunch they've brought from home. A few larger studios have a cafeteria and serve a daily lunch that's subsidized, or even free, for employees.

In general, game companies aren't strict about when you come and go. Some studios have "core hours" when teams are required to be in the office, but, like many knowledge work jobs, it's normal to leave your desk throughout the day to get coffee or a snack, to talk to a teammate about something you're working on, or to use the restroom. As long as you're getting your work done on time, you can structure your day in whatever way helps you work comfortably and productively.

When you first start a new job, you can always ask your manager and teammates what they expect of you. I've found that it's best to get to the office on the early side until you get comfortable and learn the studio culture and expectations.

Do game teams have a lot of meetings?

People like to complain about "too many meetings," but that's just because meetings can be boring. Most developers actually spend the majority of their day doing their core jobs — artists plan and create game art, programmers write and debug source code, designers write documentation and script the game levels, and producers plan out their fantasy football drafts (just kidding, producers).

Most game teams have a "stand up" meeting together each morning, especially teams that use Scrum as their development method. At the stand up, each member of the team tells about what they accomplished the day before, what they're going to accomplish today, and any problems that might be blocking their progress. After that, everybody goes back to their desks to answer email, plan their day, and work on the game.

Throughout the day, there may be additional meetings between the game team's subgroups, usually to make additional plans or decisions about specific areas of the game. For example, they might meet to collectively decide what the characters should look like, or how a particular game system should be coded, or to assess how the team is tracking against their project schedule. They have occasional play-through meetings where parts of the team plays areas of the game that were completed recently, and then talk about which areas might still be missing or may need improvement.

At the end of the day, maybe around 7:00 p.m., people start ending their workdays and going home for the night. (Unless the team is in "crunch time," then they might have dinner and get back to work.)

Game development is a team sport, and it doesn't go smoothly unless everybody's running the same playbook. Meetings can be annoying if you'd prefer to just be coding all day, but they're the best way to quickly make sure the entire team is working in the right direction.

How can I stay healthy while spending all day on a computer?

The guy who asked me this was twenty-one years old, and already having spine problems. His issues may or may not have been caused by sitting at a computer all day, but I can empathize because I've struggled with back problems and I know other game devs have too. It's been interesting to see the tactics people come up with to feel better, or at least avoid feeling worse — everything from standing desks, to inflatable Pilates ball chairs, to regularly visiting massage clinics or chiropractors. And back problems are just the beginning — there are a number of "office worker" health issues that can spring up if you're not thoughtful about staying healthy.

I'm not a doctor, and I'm definitely not qualified to diagnose health issues or prescribe solutions, but I've spent years working in game studios on a computer. I can tell you what I've seen work, and you can do your own research and talk to your doctor before trying anything. Do we have a deal?

For starters, pay attention to what you eat and how much you eat. When I got my first full-time job at a game studio, it took just a few short months to pack on an extra fifteen pounds. And it wasn't just me, it happened to so many people when they get their first game job, we even had a name for it: the Freshman Fifteen (as in, fifteen pounds). It's due to a combination of sitting all day, and eating more calories from the fully-stocked snack kitchen offered by most game studios. Plus, when a game team works long hours just before an important milestone date, managers often entice them to work after dinner by ordering high-calorie restaurant food. Long hours of no activity, plus high-calorie food and frequent snacking, equals a recipe for rapid weight gain.

So, what's a good solution? It won't be easy at first, but you could start by placing yourself on a "no snack" policy. Zero tolerance. It will test your willpower, because those snacks look delicious — especially when you're having an after-lunch blood sugar crash. But your waistline will thank you. Bring your own lunch and dinner to the office whenever you work late, because it's sure to be healthier than whatever the managers order for you.

You should also make sure your workstation is set up ergonomically, to avoid repetitive stress injuries from typing and using a mouse, and prevent muscle soreness from sitting with a bad posture. When you're typing, your elbows should be level with your wrists, and your chair should be at a height that lets your feet rest flat on the floor with your thighs roughly parallel to the ground. Your monitor should be at a height and distance that lets you view it without craning your neck into a weird position. If you search online for "workstation ergonomics," you'll find detailed instructions.

There's something else I recommend, something that you should do when you're away from your desk: exercise. Exercise is a healthy habit for most anyone, but talk to your doctor before starting a new exercise program. That said, there are so many fun ways to exercise, from jogging, to playing sports, to taking classes like yoga or martial arts (personally, my hobbies are snowboarding and parkour). The key is to find an activity that you truly enjoy doing, and then turn it into a lifelong hobby so you'll look forward to it rather than dreading it. That's my secret for staying fit, even after twenty years at a desk job.

How can I become a top performer?

Every manager is on the lookout for "rock stars." Rock stars are people who are talented, productive, amplify the productivity of their teams, and are a blast to work with. They're on a trajectory toward greatness.

Are you a rock star? If you haven't been making games for long, then you probably don't have enough experience to know how you compare to your peers. But it's never too soon to start thinking and behaving like a top performer, so let's discuss. What do top performers look like?

First, they're highly productive. And I don't mean just double the work output of other people, I'm talking as much as ten times the output of an average performer. (I'm not exaggerating — this is backed up by years of data.) Of course, they rarely get paid ten times as much, so it's obvious why companies are on the prowl for high performers: they're great bang-for-buck. You probably aren't ten times more productive than your peers just yet, but you can start paying attention to how you work and how much you get done. Start optimizing your time and your workflows and, over time, you'll be able to get more done than everybody else.

Next, top performers are highly results-focused. Do you constantly look for ways to improve your product and your team, and then just do it...or do you wait for somebody else to tell you what to do? Self-motivated people push the boundaries, and always look for ways to improve themselves and their teams. They never say "that's not my job," because they know their job is to contribute in any way they can. Take ownership of the end product, and do whatever it takes to make it awesome. That's how you deliver great results and become a top performer.

What if I'm not an expert in anything?

If you're just starting your game dev career, you've probably learned a bit about a wide variety of skills, tools, and technologies, but you haven't yet gone "deep" into any specific areas. That's a great foundation, but to stand out from the crowd you need to offer something that everyone else does *not* have — you need to be an expert in a particular art technique, or a particular design tool, or a particular area of technology.

If that sounds intimidating, then I'll let you in on a key secret: "expert" is a relative term. You don't need to be better than everybody, you only need to be better than the other people in your peer group. So if you're better than the other game developers applying for the same jobs as you at the same level, then you're sure to stand out from the crowd.

How do you know if you're better? Well, usually, there's no way to find out ahead of time. Just put in the work to get as good as you can at the skills you need, and follow your curiosity to invest more time and effort in areas that interest you. If you're a programmer, maybe it's graphics or physics. For an artist, maybe it's character animation. For game designers, maybe it's the nuances of constructing an engaging game level. Whatever it is, if you put in more effort than your peers, then you're likely to be the one who gets the job offer — because you're the expert.

How can I find a career mentor?

My career in the game industry has been an amazing journey. But I wasn't always a wizened old game industry veteran — there was a time, back when I was taking my own first baby steps toward a new career, when I had no idea where I was going or how to get there (or, honestly, what my life might be like when I arrived). My path was meandering and unpredictable, and it sometimes felt like the failures outnumbered the successes.

But I learned a lot along the way. Much of the time, my lessons were acquired through the painful brute force of trial and error. But there were also people in my life who helped steer me in the right direction by offering advice, coaching, support and friendship. I often didn't realize at the time how much I needed them, but looking back now, I can see clearly that their care and support wasn't just "nice to have" — it was, in fact, the single biggest influence driving me forward every step of the way.

Whether it's a friend, co-worker, manager, significant other — or even somebody you only know through their blogs, books, and podcasts — I can't overemphasize how important it is for you to seek mentorship throughout your career. And mentorships don't have to be "formal," because they rarely are. Most of the time, it's just a matter of seeking advice from people in your life who know you and care about your success, and might have a little wisdom or insight to help you through your next challenge.

If you're lucky, you'll find several informal mentors over the years, and each of them will have a slightly different take on your life and your situation. For example, a parent may understand you in one way, whereas a manager at work may understand you in a different way. Each of them is likely to have reasonable advice, but it's up to you to take it all in, filter it through the lens of your own skills, talents, and career goals, and then make your own decision on how to move forward.

In short, mentors are everywhere. Start by looking around you for people who are older than you, or have been doing the work longer than you, or who come from a different background than you and can provide a unique perspective. Tell them your situation, ask for their advice, and then listen to it with an open mind — with the understanding that it's just one person's perspective for you to consider. And remember to say thanks.

Additional wisdom and inspiration

This book dispenses a truckload of career advice, but I certainly don't corner the market on game industry wisdom. So here are some bite-sized yet insightful words from the smart, talented game developers I've interviewed over the years. Visit GameIndustryCareerGuide.com to read the full interviews.

"Start simple and learn from others. Before you know it, you will be creating some pretty cool stuff!"
Brandon Fogerty, Graphics Programmer

"Go and make games. It doesn't matter if you finish the project. (Guess what? You probably won't.)"
Dan Posluns, Game Programmer

"Make sure you love it. Draw every day. Play the beautiful games before you play the fun ugly ones."
Caleb Parrish, Environment Artist

"It has to be in your blood. Draw SOMETHING every day! Even if it is just some quick doodles on a napkin."
Rich Werner, 2D Artist/Animator

"Make your own games. Small ones, if necessary. The world is full of great tools for burgeoning game writers and designers, so just dive in and make a little game. This will look incredibly impressive to a prospective employer."
Darby McDevitt, Game Writer

"If you fully invest yourself in any trade it can be incredibly draining, but also quite rewarding when you see the final product."
Tyler Finney, Concept Artist

"It is that magic moment when you look at the screen and it becomes a

'real game' for the first time."
Tamara Knoss, Lead UI Artist

"Getting to do a final mix for a game, and realizing it sounds like what you've been imagining in your head for months (or years, in some cases) is one of my happiest work and artistic moments."
Jaclyn Shumate, Sound Designer

"It's awesome to see all the hard work come to fruition and have evidence that it's having an impact on players!"
Diana Hsu, Product Manager

"I can't tell you how many times I got told no. It just makes me try harder every time someone says I can't do something. Find a way."
Kris Durrschmidt, Indie Game Developer

"Each rejection I received motivated me to work harder until I was eventually able to get my foot in the door of a game studio."
Tony Ravo, Character Animator

"Fight every day to stay afloat. Do everything you can to stand out in the crowd. Keep perfecting your craft every chance you get, and you will eventually get there."
Ted Wennerstrom, Game Audio Freelancer

"Be inspired, believe in yourself. There's a lot to learn to impress yourself, and even more to impress others."
Darran Hurlbut, Character Artist

"Don't let a misguided belief of 'It's too late' or 'I can't do it' keep you from the video game industry. You have one life to live, and the worst thing you can ever do is get to the end of it and regret never trying."
Jason Van Beveren, Community Manager

"Start! Nothing should stop you from doing design right now. Go make a game. You don't need a programmer, you don't need an artist, you just need yourself and some paper and you can start designing."
Kelly Toyama, Game Designer

"I get asked all the time: How do you get into the game industry? My answer is always: Why aren't you already in the game industry right now? Go make something. Anything."

Frank Rogan, Senior Producer

Now is your time for action

Now that you've read this book, what will you do with everything you've learned? What's the next step in your own video game career?

Whatever you do, don't procrastinate — take action starting now. Ride this wave of inspiration. Because the sooner you get started, the sooner you'll build the world's next exciting, beautiful, immersive, epic, quirky, terrifying, hilarious, awe-inspiring, uniquely-yours video game of tomorrow. And the sooner you create it, the sooner I can play it.

I can't wait!

About the author

Jason W. Bay is the creator of the Game Industry Career Guide website, where he publishes insider information and inspiration to help thousands of aspiring game developers start and build their careers.

Jason has spent over fifteen years in the video game industry in many roles including tester, designer, writer, programmer, technical director, product manager, and studio head. He's been a featured presenter at international game industry conferences, written for industry magazines, and worked with top game development schools to help students get hired.

Connect with Jason on Twitter @YourGameCareer, or swing by his career website for a ton of free info about game industry jobs at: GameIndustryCareerGuide.com.

Also by Jason W. Bay

Thank you for reading this book! If you liked it, please help me spread the word by telling people about it, sharing it with your friends, and consider writing a review online.

Other things I made for you:

Land a Job as a Video Game Tester
   "…an excellent, probably indispensable, tool for the fledgling tester."

Game Industry Career Guide Podcast
   "Full of juicy bits and info on how to apply, how to get ready, how to build your portfolio and tons more."

GameIndustryCareerGuide.com
   "…please NEVER abandon your website, it has helped and influenced me and so many others."

Credits

Cover design
Jason W. Bay

Author photo
Yee Feng

Copy editing
Shannon Page

Special thanks to:
Brad Lansford, Brandon Fogerty, Caleb Parrish, Crazy Viking Studios, Dominic Sodano, Katie Orcutt, Mark Ferrari, Mathias Takacs, Randy Briley, Steve Vallée, and many other talented game developers and managers who supported, inspired, and guided me throughout my career. I'm paying it forward. Thank you!

23279232R00072

Printed in Great Britain
by Amazon